PRACTICAL PROFILING

MOYRA EVANS

ROUTLEDGE
London

First published in 1988 by
Routledge
a division of Routledge, Chapman and Hall
11 New Fetter Lane, London EC4P 4EE

Published in the USA by
Routledge
a division of Routledge, Chapman and Hall, Inc.
29 West 35th Street, New York NY 10001

Printed and bound in Great Britain by
Biddles Ltd, Guildford and King's Lynn

British Library Cataloguing in Publication Data

Evans, M.M.
 Practical profiling.
 1. Students — Great Britain — Rating of
 2. Education, Secondary — Great Britain
 I. Title
 373.12′7   LB1117

ISBN 0-415-00544-2

CONTENTS

TABLES

Tables

ACKNOWLEDGEMENTS

I should like to thank all the staff of Glenthorne High School for Girls who contributed to the process of profiling and to the end product of our First Year Record of Achievement. In particular, I should like to acknowledge the contributions made by the Working Party in thinking through the ideas; by the INSET working party for thinking about and planning the in-service activities and by Mrs K. Pullen and Ms V. Porritt for the Case Studies and departmental policy on assessment in Chapter Five.

I am also grateful for the support and encouragement of the Head Teacher, Mrs V. Barkey.

PREFACE

It should be noted, that, as the school in which this work was developed is a girls' school, most of the text uses the female subject and pronoun. This is not intended to imply any peripheralisation of the male of the species to profiling.

As it is a case study of a particular school, and many of the activities were undertaken by several people, I have referred to them through the collective 'we'. Where I refer to 'I', my intention was to reflect my own thoughts or activities.

Chapter One

RECORDS OF ACHIEVEMENT - CAN THEY WORK?

We are ... faced with an entirely new situation where the goal of education, if we are to survive, is the facilitation of change and learning. The only man who is educated is the man who has learned how to learn; the man who has learned to adapt and change; the man who has realised that no knowledge is secure, that only the process of seeking knowledge gives a base for security. Changingness, a reliance on process rather than upon static knowledge, is the only thing that makes sense as a goal for education in the modern world. (Carl Rogers, 1969, Freedom to learn; a view of what education might become).

The focus of this book is on processes; the process of thinking about profiles, of looking at the variety of ideas which could be put to work, of trying things out, of showing that they do not always work, of making decisions, of making the best use of the restricted resources at our disposal, but most of all it is about the process of introducing a quite radical idea into a school which has up till now thrived on traditionalist beliefs. It is a description of how we set about introducing Records of Achievement to our First Year pupils and it is a story which will include 'warts and all', because, despite much careful thought which we hoped would lead us directly to a 'good' outcome, we can now see that such a finite state does not exist, that what is good to one person is not so good to another, and that the 'outcome' will be constantly subject to revision. So this is a story of processes; and it is through the *process* that we learn how to improve what we have achieved, just as it is

1

the process of profiling which is, or should be, far more important to our pupils than the summative documents.

This takes us back to the quotation from Carl Rogers who points to the fact that 'no knowledge is secure, that only the process of seeking knowledge gives a base for security'. The more involved we become in the profiling process the more we realise that there are no perfect answers to the problems which undoubtedly occur; that there is no absolute truth other than the constant moving forwards of our thoughts and therefore, hopefully, of our practice.

THE BACKGROUND

At our school, Records of Achievement had their origin in a wish to review the end of year reports sent home to parents for all Lower School (first to third year) pupils. Until July 1985, these were dispatched from school to home, via the pupil, in a sealed envelope, and the child usually had no knowledge of the contents of her report. In July 1987, instead of a report, First Year pupils took home a Record of Achievement which they had negotiated with their teachers, and which they had read on its completion in school. Instead of being an unknown statement from school to home, the pupils had made a major contribution to the document and it belonged to them. This represented a considerable shift of emphasis over the developmental period of the previous twelve months.

The case study school is a nonselective, five form entry, 11-18 girls' school in an outer London Borough. The Head Teacher had been in post since September 1982, and had already introduced many changes into the school before any work was started on Records of Achievement. The early changes had included a major review of the curriculum, with departments looking in detail at their aims and objectives; organisation of pupil groups for teaching purposes; end of year reports and norm referenced grades; the house system and so on. During the last three years, (1984-7) the Certificate of Pre-Vocational Education (CPVE), the Technical and Vocational Educational Initiative (TVEI), the School Mathematics Project (SMP) 11-16, the modular curriculum and of course, the General Certificate of Secondary Education (GCSE) have all arrived at the school. So it is a school which is used to change, although until quite recently, the emphasis has always been on traditional approaches to teaching and learning. Provision of INSET to support TVEI and GCSE, borough support for innovation in mathematics teaching, together with new arrangements for organising INSET in schools generally, have all contributed to a recent, perceptible shift in teaching methods.

One of the other significant strands in supporting a climate in which it has been possible to introduce Records of Achievement has been the development of the pastoral system. As this gathers momentum teachers begin to feel that it is not compatible with subjective judgements being handed down to children without allowing them the right of reply, it is not compatible with labelling children as failures because they find academic work hard and it is not compatible with attempting to spoon feed knowledge into children. An effective pastoral system encourages teachers to question important issues such as the part children play in their own learning, the consideration which should exist between teacher and taught and vice versa, and the quality of classroom relationships in general. It also seems inappropriate to compare children with others in their groups; the pastoral system is concerned with the individual child, and with developing her self-esteem. John Holt, in his book 'How Children Fail' (1965), warned against destroying the wish to learn in children by

> compelling them to work for petty and contemptible rewards - gold stars or papers marked 100 and tacked to the wall, or as on report cards, or honour rolls ... - in short, for the ignoble satisfaction of feeling that they are better than someone else. We encourage them to feel that the end and aim of all they do in school is nothing more than to get a good mark on a test, or to impress someone with what they seem to know.

To be compared with others can seem invidious to the individual, who after all, can only be herself; she can make a greater or lesser effort; she can achieve high or low results, but, in the long run, it is in comparing herself today with what she could do or did do some time previously that she can assess how she feels about herself, and it is in setting targets as a result of this insight that she can become involved in what she hopes for her future. We are moving towards an understanding that how a person feels should be taken into account in education; that 'knowing things' is not

3

sufficient. Affective learning - learning to recognise, understand and deal with feelings - is as important as cognitive development in moving individuals towards personal autonomy and it has significant implications for the way in which children are taught and assessed in school.

In considering whether a school is ready to take on Records of Achievement, it is interesting to look at its organisational climate and its prevailing pedagogic styles. W.K. Hoy and C.G. Miskel (1978) have defined an organisational climate as 'that set of internal character-istics which distinguishes one school from another, and which influences the behaviour of people in each school'. A. Halpin (1967), said that he 'began with the obvious analogy that personality is to the human individual as "organisational climate" is to the organisation', whilst E. Hoyle (1986) was concerned with the quality of relationships between people within the organisation. I would venture to suggest that the individual characteristics of a school are largely determined by the management style of the person within the school, whether Head or Deputy, who wields the power, by the relationships which flourish as a consequence and by the structures which are set up to enable the school to function as an organisation.

A. Halpin's study (1966) of organisational climate was based on the perceived behaviour of the head teacher - namely, aloofness, production emphasis, thrust and consideration, and the resultant perceived behaviour of the teachers - disengagement, hindrance, esprit and intimacy. From his work he disclosed that the 'profiles clustered into six groups' (Hughes, Ribbens and Thomas, 1985) from which he invented six climates along a continuum from 'closed' to 'open'. The significant features of these climates are that the '*open* climate is characterised by 'authenticity on the part of the principal and staff; the principal leading by example and the staff showing commitment and working well together, so that acts of leadership emerge naturally as needed. The *closed* climate is in stark contrast; the principal provides no effective leadership and is preoccupied with formalities and trivia, while the teachers are frustrated and apathetic, responding at a minimal level' (Hughes et. al. ibid).

There follow case studies of two fictitious schools which have been designed to show the extremes of organisational climate so that the everyday reality of each may be felt.

Case Study 1

Evergreen School. Mrs Keene, the Head Teacher, was at her desk at 7.30 am as usual, having left her family slumbering fitfully. She never stopped to wonder whether perhaps the day would come when they stayed in bed instead of getting themselves off to school. She trusted them and she knew they responded to that trust. She was that sort of a person. She expected certain things to happen and as far as anyone could see, they always did.

She removed last night's paper work from her briefcase and organised it in appropriate piles around her desk. If its particular pile wasn't dealt with by the end of the day, then it went home for reconsideration, and turned up in a different spot the next morning, in the hope of achieving a higher priority.

A colleague popped in to discuss an idea with her, and eventually went away confident that she could continue to develop it. By assembly time, Mrs Keene had talked to various members of staff and was happy that the ideas spinning around were all holding their own in the great juggling act that she felt she had set going. She chatted to the teacher who had taken assembly about one particular aspect of it that had interested her. That was one of the good things about Mrs Keene - she usually found lots of things to interest her as the day went by.

Meanwhile, staff were making their way to their rooms where classes were to be found getting their books ready to start the lesson. Mrs Keene was reminded of the practice in her last school of how the children used to slide their expensive bags across the playground, and then rush after them for the re-throw. There was none of that at Evergreen School thank goodness! The wear and tear on the bags was tremendous, as it had been also on her good humour. Here at Evergreen, she was pleased to say, time-wasting activities were only noticeable by their absence; children got down to work quickly because their teachers expected it of them and because lessons were usually engaging.

Mrs Keene had a great capacity for talking to people and for being interested in other people's points of view. She helped staff to probe their own ideas and they knew that the structures she had set up for communication in the school usually worked because of the goodwill they felt was present in the school. There were always the few, however, who had an axe to grind, and who complained about yet another sheet of paper, or yet another meeting, or 'why can't I get on with teaching them the basics, instead of trying out these fancy ideas!' Nobody really had too much time to take any notice of these, so they grumbled away amongst themselves. The rest of the staff spent their time rushing between the typewriter, the photocopier, the classroom, the individual child and the meetings, and from time to time wondered if, like the hamster in the biology laboratory, they would ever be able to get off the 'exercise wheel'. They also wondered where the general public had picked up the idea of the 9–3.30 teacher.

Case Study 2

Downland View School. The Head, Mr Ake, was not a well person. He was much concerned with his various health problems. Many of his staff had been at the school since before his time, and the others were youngsters, just arrived from college. The younger members of staff often met for a drink in the evenings, or went out somewhere together, like to the football at Anfield. The older ones had settled into a comfortable routine of leisure interests, e.g. golf, gardening or moonlighting. Mr Ake did not make many demands of them in school, but, on the other hand, if they wanted to burden themselves with school work, that was perfectly all right by him, just so long as they did not demand any really positive interest to be shown in it.

Mr Ake was quite good with words, and used to sit in his room thinking for long periods of time. He used to come up with some lengthy memos covering his responsibility to the LEA, which from time to time bombarded him with things to organise. The office bought an electric paper shredder to deal with all the classified 'D' notice information sheets with which they had to deal.

From time to time, Mr Ake was sufficiently bothered by an incident or complaint that he gathered the staff together and told them that they should really be working harder to prevent such things from happening, although he could see that life was very difficult and there really wasn't much that one could do. He certainly didn't have the answers. He was fond of remarking that perhaps 'our critics should come and teach in order to find out what things were like'.

Alas! Tragedy struck the usual tranquility of existence

at Downland View School. Unknown to anyone at school, Mr Ake had been negotiating for early retirement and succeeded in his claim. The immediate outcome of this was for the staff to eagerly investigate whether they too could find any just cause for early retirement, but on ascertaining that this would be unlikely, they fell to discussing which one of them should apply for Mr Ake's job, on the grounds that they were as capable as he was of sitting behind a closed door and writing copious and unnecessary notes to staff.

However, the question one or two teachers were asking was, how could a new head, when appointed, succeed in changing the climate of this school from one where few teachers had any real interest in children and their education, to one where the atmosphere was such that both children and staff were eager to go each day.

I am sure most teachers with experience at different schools could identify the types of climate existing at Evergreen and Downland View Schools, and could further recognise that the quality of the relationships is consequent upon the management style of the Head Teacher. At Evergreen there is a feeling of task fulfilment both on the part of the teachers and from the pupils' point of view, and it is clear that much of the observed behaviour is expected, but not taken for granted. People also are not taken for granted, and obviously feel they can talk freely about their ideas and develop them. They are involved in ideas, so it is a school where thinking is valued. It should, therefore, be able to support new ideas and to think its way around the problems which crop up in any developing initiative.

Downland View, on the other hand, is a school where much of the teachers' energies are spent in activities outside school hours. It is an environment where no-one shows a great deal of interest in professional development or in talking about ideas; it lacks the busy feel of Evergreen, and presents a 'closed door', disinterested scenario. Teachers do not work together with any feeling of cohesion, because there is a lack of enthusiastic guidance, and a lack of expectation that they should do anything other than be in lessons teaching children.

Evergreen represents the 'open' end of Halpin's organisational climate, whilst Downland View falls somewhere towards the closed end of the continuum. It is clear from our case studies that an innovation such as

Records of Achievement is much more likely to be nurtured and to survive in an open organisational climate where teachers are encouraged to think, to talk, and to try things out, than in the closed climate.

It is not only the organisational climate but also the style of the pedagogy which must to a certain extent determine whether a school could support the introduction of Records of Achievement. E. Hoyle (1986) has defined pedagogy as 'the process by which knowledge and skills are transmitted through class teaching and through the informal processes of teaching and learning'.

Most schools are staffed by teachers who display a range of pedagogic styles from traditional didactic teaching at one end of the continuum to student-centred learning at the other extreme. A.V. Kelly (1986), in his book 'Knowledge and Curriculum Planning', has drawn together the philosophical arguments for these extremes and this provides us with an interesting insight into the diversity of teaching style. Kelly describes how the epistemological debate on the nature of truth, knowledge and values, polarises into rationalist and empiricist perspectives of education. Rationalism - deriving from Plato originally, then the German philosophers, Immanuel Kant, Georg Hegel and others, and more recently developed by Richard Peters (1965) - is concerned with explaining things through the mind and thus through rationality, giving little credence to understanding life through the senses.

> (Rationalism) offers a strong view of 'truth', sees large areas of knowledge as being certain, or at least potentially certain, regards knowledge for the most part as propositional - as 'knowledge that', and believes that justification can be found for assertions of value - moral, aesthetic, and educational - in reason itself, in the concept of the rational mind. (Kelly, ibid).

Kelly points to the fact that the rationalist perspective in education is strongly concerned with knowledge and the content of subjects; with the academic and the intellectual, and with ascribing value hierarchically to subjects. It sees the affective development of the individual as rather insignificant, thus taking little account of the feelings associated with cognitive learning.

The empiricist perspective challenges this view of rationality and values. Empiricism embraces the 'experience of the senses' and claims that subject content is of secondary importance to the facilitation of the growth and development of each child. It does not see knowledge as certain and unchanging, but it does see it as

> a means of coming to learn, to understand and to think; and it believes that no kind of ultimate justification of an objective kind can be found for any assertions of value, that values are relative, man-made, socially constructed. (Kelly, ibid).

The empiricist view of education was the basis of J. Dewey's experiential approach to children's learning; empiricism takes account of children's experiences, commonsense knowledge, and emotional development. It stresses the process of guided growth and participation rather than outcomes, and it stresses the changeability of values rather than the certainty of what is right and good. It thus supports the Carl Rogers' statement which began this chapter, that 'a reliance on process rather than static knowledge, is the only thing which makes sense as a goal for education in the modern world'. It is the philosophical basis for John Holt's beliefs (op.cit.) when he talked of teachers failing children through 'making them afraid of ... making mistakes, of failing, of being wrong'; and of his discussion on the curriculum and the value ascribed to traditional subjects. In his strong plea for a different approach to teaching, he said,

> Since we can't know what knowledge will be most needed in future, it is senseless to try to teach it in advance. Instead, we should try to turn out people who love learning so much and learn so well that they will be able to learn whatever needs to be learned.

As we move on to discuss the theoretical aspects of Records of Achievement, it will be seen that their philosophical base is located in empiricism rather than rationalism, and this has considerable implications for the style of pedagogy which needs to be adopted. Pedagogy based on empiricism, values students as people who are capable of developing their own thinking, and recognises that they come to lessons with a measure of knowledge and experience. Teachers working from this philosophical base approach their lessons with the intention that children should be active in their learning; that games and discussion form a valued part of the learning process (Bruner, 1966, Bullock, 1975); that group work and role play contribute to the development of thought, cooperation and empathy; and that self-assessment forms an important part of the personal development of the student. Thus classrooms where such learning is taking place are characterised by the democratic relationship between teacher and taught; by acceptance of tentative statements and attempts at self expression; by the active involvement of pupils and a feeling of ownership of their ideas and the substance of their ideas. The pedagogy is one of facilitation rather than imposition; it is one of support where the teacher aims to be non-judgemental; it is one where feelings are accepted and attempts are made to understand them; it is one where pupils' thinking will be moved on by active learning methods, by talking through ideas and by working cooperatively rather than competitively.

Most schools contain a considerable mix of teaching styles, and any shift in methodology represents an adventurous step into the unknown for the teacher who might have been used to formal teaching for many years. As B. MacDonald (1973a) said, 'Genuine innovation begets incompetence. It deskills teacher and pupil alike, suppressing acquired competencies and demanding the development of new ones.' So it is small wonder that teachers feel threatened by innovation, as they know there is safety in what they feel they have always done successfully.

However, many secondary school teachers have experienced, to a greater or lesser degree, the recent developments in the pastoral programme in the form of active tutorial work; changes in teaching styles to cope with GCSE; and the experiential learning associated with TVEI. These developments, supported by a certain amount of INSET, have been paving the way for pedagogic development to suit both the climate of the school, and the initiatives which are introduced into it.

At the other extreme from formal teaching on the teaching methodology continuum is student-centred learning, and this is consistent with the process of recording achievement, and indeed they tend to reinforce each other. Inherent to student-centred learning is the process of self-assessment and recording what the child can do; and conversely if records of achievement are introduced in the school, many teachers will want to move towards these kinds of teaching methods. This does not mean to say that records of achievement will be unsuccessful unless all teachers are completely student-centred; but rather it does seem that a move away from formal teaching methods is fairly essential as a starting point. Formal teaching, based on rationalism, values subject content above the process of learning, but recording achievement is concerned with developing the skill of becoming more self aware through learning to assess oneself, and as such stresses the process involved in learning. There is a different emphasis on what is happening in the learning - in the one case it is to do with the content of what is learnt, but in the other, the stress is on how the learning is achieved.

One of the biggest problems in bringing change to a school is that, for it eventually to be effective, attitudes of teachers also have to change. An understanding of the philosophical issues on which the change is based will help to bring about fundamental rethinking so that the change will be less likely to be purely superficial. In the case of records of achievement, unless it is understood that the process is all-important, there will be quite critical problems in implementing it because teachers will be concerned over the loss of teaching time, and therefore will be worried about their inability to complete the syllabus. If, on the other hand, the move in thinking takes up the desirability of the process, then covering subject content becomes less of a problem.

Real change cannot happen overnight, nor will it occur unless various factors are present, not least motivation on the part of the teacher. A carefully planned INSET programme helps, but it needs to be set in the context of a supportive, forward looking and considerate organisational climate. Much of the literature on innovation stresses that not only is it a matter of providing teachers with new information, but also that attitudes, beliefs, and values may need to be rethought (Taylor, 1982; Havelock R, Guskin, Frohman, Havelock M, Hill and Huber, 1973). For this to come about, time is needed, and patience on the part of the innovator(s) to let ideas ferment and to provide appropriate settings for them to be discussed. A further determinant in how committed teachers will eventually be to changes, is how much they feel they are involved in the deliberations and planning that needs to go on prior to their introduction.

There are numerous barriers to the introduction of

changes, many of which have been identified by Telfer (1977) as follows: 'lack of time, lack of effective means of communication, lack of agreement about what is to be done, lack of money to do the necessary tasks, staff turnover, poor teacher preparation, lack of teacher interest and cooperation, lack of top-level administration support and teacher apathy'. This forms an impressive list, from which teachers with experience of innovating will immediately recognise some as having impeded their own progress! No doubt some of these barriers are present to a degree in any innovating situation, and especially so in schools where resources are constantly stretched. If we look at the nature of the barriers, however, it is probably true that the school whose organisational climate is towards the open end of the continuum will have fewer of these problems to contend with than that of a school at the closed end.

EARLY DAYS

Our project began in the summer term of 1986, when informal discussions took place with various members of staff on the general topic of reports, and in particular, the interim report, which was known as the progress report, consisting of one A4 sheet of brief comments from subject and form teachers. It was given to parents on the consultation evening, and had to be returned at the end of the evening so that it could be filed for reference. The system seemed unsatisfactory in various ways. Firstly, the staff felt that since most parents came in to see them on that evening, it was a duplication of effort for them to have to write down what they could perfectly well say to the parent face to face. Secondly, the parents had little time to digest the contents of the report before speaking to teachers about their comments. It could be assumed that much which might have been said after careful thought went unremarked because of the lack of preparation on the part of the parents, through no fault of their own. Thirdly, this time factor implied a lack of involvement on the part of the pupil because she was neither consulted over what was written, nor was she able to put forward her point of view to her parent before parent-teacher discussion took place. The power in the discussion dynamics, therefore, was rather heavily weighted in favour of the teacher. Some people might have felt this was quite in order, but such a way of going on fails to take account of the fact that if the teacher wants the child to improve her performance in some respect, the pupil needs to feel that she is a key figure in the negotiations. She clearly was not if no one ever asked for her point of view.

Fourthly, the fact that the parent had to surrender the report at the end of the evening meant that it could not be taken home to be thought about further, and, of course, the pupil, about whom staff had written certain statements, never had the opportunity of reading what had been said. So the children whose teachers were pleased with their progress and said so, did not have the satisfaction of seeing this; they were merely given a potted version of what the parent could remember. Parents tend to remember some things more easily than others, and it is often the less good comments which seem to stick in the memory. Some parents also have misguided notions of not telling their children how well they have done for fear of making them 'big-headed'. Equally importantly, the children whose progress did not seem to be satisfactory only heard what their parents told them; one wonders how useful this was in the context of helping them to improve their attitude, effort, presentation, concentration or whatever was causing the problem. Finally we are left with the parent who was unable to attend the evening - very few in number as most of them were interested in their child's progress and were able to show this by attending. All of those who did not come were contacted by the school; most were sorry to have missed the evening but were prevented by particular circumstances from doing so. However, it was not customary for the school to send a duplicate report home, so these parents, and, in particular, their children, missed out on getting essential feedback on their progress.

As a result of the discussions on progress reports the Head Teacher decided it would be appropriate to set up a working party to look at them, to see how other teachers felt about them and to see whether we could come up with an alternative approach. At this time, she and I discussed Records of Achievement in principle, as a possible development of the thinking of the working party, but the brief was really only to look at the progress reports.

The idea of a working party was appealing for a variety of reasons. It would be small, thus allowing individuals to make useful contributions. An important part of the planning was to decide on the composition of the group so that a wide cross-section of interests would be included. Problems associated with asking people to go on a working party include the fact that others with a particular interest might be overlooked by mistake; and that those who are asked but would prefer not to have been, might feel they cannot decline in the interests of maintaining diplomatic relationships with the senior staff. On the other hand, asking for volunteers is a risky business as the final group dynamics may prove to be unsatisfactory, or there may be an imbalance of interest factors, or people may be reluctant to suggest themselves for a host of different reasons. We eventually decided that the group should comprise representatives from English and expressive arts, mathematics, modern languages, humanities, science, information technology, physical education, special educational needs, tutorial work and art/pottery/home economics/needlework. These people were then asked by the Head if they would be interested in taking part; her involvement at this stage lent authority and moral support for the venture which could be clearly seen by the participants. Their status ranged from a scale one teacher, through scales two and three to scale four. With this sort of mixture, it was hoped to gather a range of opinion from teachers at different developmental stages of their careers and with different responsibilities. Obviously status influences the way teachers experience the structures of the organisation and it was important for this to be accounted for.

Following the first meeting the group gelled quite happily (see C. Handy (1976) for an interesting discourse on the working of groups). We discussed the task and how we could open the debate amongst our colleagues. To begin with the group was concerned with gathering information on how other teachers felt about the progress reports and whether any suggestions were forthcoming for improvements; then we discussed our own thoughts and suggestions as well, and came to some decisions. We decided that we needed a report for the consultation evening which would open a dialogue; that we did not need it to be as detailed as previously; that we could therefore use a code to identify different comments; and that we wanted to be able to store the information we had listed.

So basing our design on that of a progress report from a school in the Midlands which we thought was quite succinct, we talked through what we liked and did not like about it.

The comments on the report were as follows:

good progress and substantial effort   G
satisfactory effort and progress   S
disappointing progress despite conscientious work   M
insufficient progress   P
unsatisfactory effort   X
unsatisfactory effort and insufficient progress   U

We particularly liked the choice of symbols which we felt were not value laden as A, B or C might have been, but we also thought that we would prefer a version like that in Table 1.1 as this gave more versatility to the comments.

A 'mix and match' operation could be performed and a section on homework could be added; but it will be immediately observed that our example in Table 1.1 had reverted to traditional symbols. Part of this we changed before the production of the first version of the new progress report, as can be seen in Table 1.2.

The production of the progress report was our first task as a group and represented our first incursion into the thorny path of trying to find the 'right' words to express concepts which each person understood slightly differently according to the attitudes, values, and beliefs of his or her perception of reality. This in part also depended on how much thought had been given to the type of statements teachers wanted to make about children - whether they felt happy with expressing negative comments if, in their opinion, they considered them to be true; whether they felt it is right to draw attention to the child's lack of ability; whether they felt that positive statements only should be made; whether they felt children ever deserve the highest praise; and whether they felt there is no problem in making subjective judgments on children.

It should be remembered that the idea of this progress report was to communicate with the home so that discussion could be started on how to help the pupil in the immediate future. It was really intended as a quick way of presenting and storing information and could never provide the comprehensive coverage which a more detailed report could have done. So it had considerable limitations in what it was able to do, but despite those limitations we wanted to produce a document which would allow teacher and parent to begin talking in an undefensive way if this were possible. We therefore had to choose our statements with very great care, and we found that we had great difficulty in agreeing on some of them. This was probably a good sign as it meant that discussion in the working party was beginning to flow openly and the ideas and suggestions which were voiced enabled us to look at points of view which undoubtedly moved our thinking forward. C. Handy (1976) pointed to the fact that groups produce fewer ideas than individuals working separately, but they 'produce better ideas in the sense that they are better evaluated, more thought through'. It could also be said of groups working effectively that they are more motivated through interaction and group commitment to produce both the ideas and the end product, than individuals working to an already busy schedule in school.

The area which gave us the most difficulty was where a child had problems with the work, seemed to make little progress, had a history of low attainment and may have needed special help either in the past or now. This child really focussed our attention into what we should be saying about children in reports, and it seemed a matter of great importance that, whilst previously we may have been guilty individually of making bland statements regarding their progress almost without thinking twice about it, we now had to be able to express our thoughts clearly, concisely and with meaning. Also we had to be able to justify our decisions to the rest of the professional body of teachers, and this was a fairly daunting task.

In Table 1.1 we have 'LIMITED 3 (but consistent with ability)'. This was intended to indicate limited progress, but we eventually felt the word 'limited' was too value laden to use. Limited progress easily slid into being interpreted as limited ability, and whilst this was not what we wished to say, we felt it could seem that way. So 'consistent with ability' was added, but now perhaps we had fallen into another trap. Were we contributing to the self-fulfilling prophecy - namely 'we cannot expect any more of her than this'?

There was much detailed discussion on this particular issue and others as well, but eventually it was resolved temporarily by using 'needs considerable help'. 'Unsatisfactory' was also disliked because of its value judgement connotations, and 'capable of better work' was substituted in its place. This version of the report was used for First Year pupils in November 1986, and we felt considerably pressured by time in having to produce a document so relatively quickly. Following departmental evaluation after the reports had been used, we revised them as can be seen in Table 1.3.

By combining the progress and effort statements we had lost some of the versatility which we had liked in Table 1.2, but felt far more satisfied with the comments at which we eventually arrived. We also had some flexibility built into the system and advice given from the working party to the staff included the following:

It is intended that you will select from the range of statements one or two which most faithfully reflect(s) your opinion of the pupil's work and enter it/them in the column headed 'Description of Work'.

We think that the categories 'HG', 'HA' and 'S' should stand alone; as would also 'Y', which is intended to cover those pupils who are wasting time, in whatever idiosyncratic way this might be displayed. You would probably want to tick the 'appointment advised' column if you had entered 'Y'. 'T' and 'F' were designed to give staff versatility in what they might want to say, and were not intended to be used in isolation, as we do not think they give the parent sufficient information if entered on their own. Ideally they link up with 'Q'.

Only in exceptional circumstances should 'Q' be entered on its own, and if so it should be supported by a tick in the 'appointment advised' column. 'L' can be used separately, but could also fit with 'Q'. It would also be possible to enter 'QFL' if you feel this is appropriate.

Evaluation of this report showed that the comments still did not cater for all eventualities, but this was only to be expected. It did, however, fulfil its objectives in that it did act as a basis for discussion between teacher and parent, it was quick to complete, and it was possible to store on computer for reference. So it was adopted for use with each of the first three years, having a slight addition to the third year report (Table 1.4) to give a little extra information to help in choice of subjects for the fourth year.

The review of progress reports which had been the working party's brief was complete by the early part of 1987, and as a result of the thinking and talking we had engaged in about assessing children, about the fairness of teachers' comments, and about involvement of children in their own assessment, it was felt that we should move on to looking at records of achievement and how they might develop from the stage we had reached now.

Table 1.1: An Alternative Version

Progress		Effort Made		Homework	
Very Good	1	Substantial	A	Usually Done	R
Steady	2	Hard Working	B	Unreliable	U
Limited (but consistent with ability)	3	Casual	C		
Unsatisfactory (capable of better work)	4	Unsatisfactory	D		

Records of Achievement

Table 1.2

Progress Report 1

Name _____ Form _____ Date _____

Progress		Effort Made		Homework	
Very Good	1	Hard Working	H	Always Done	R
Steady	2	Steady	S	Usually Done	U
Needs considerable help	3	Casual	L	Unreliable	N
Capable of better work	4	Unsatisfactory	Y		

Subject	Teacher	Progress	Effort	Home-work	Appoint-ment
English					
Mathematics					
Science					
French					
History					
Geography					
RE					
Art					
Needlework					
Home Economics					
Music					
PE					

Signed _____ Form Teacher

Table 1.3

Progress Report 2

Name _____ Form _____ Date _____

Within her group, this pupil
HG works hard, with good results
HA works hard; making reasonable progress
S usually works well, making reasonable progress
Q needs considerable help (and)
T tries hard
F does not always try hard enough
L concentrates for short periods of time only; therefore progress is slow
Y does not make good use of time. Her work suffers as a result

Her homework is					
Always done	R	Usually done	U	Unreliable	N

Subject	Teacher	Group	Description of work	Home-work	Appointment advised
English					
Mathematics					
Science					
Biology					
French					
German					
History					
Geography					
RE					
Art					
Textiles					
Home Economics					
Music					
PE					

Signed _____ Form Teacher [   ]

Table 1.4

Third Year Progress Report

Name _____ Form _____ Date _____

	Within her group, this pupil	
HG	works hard, with good results	
HA	works hard; making reasonable progress	
S	usually works well, making reasonable progress	
Q	needs considerable help (and)	
T	tries hard	
F	does not always try hard enough	
L	concentrates for short periods of time only; therefore progress is slow	
Y	does not make good use of time. Her work suffers as a result	

Her homework is

Always done [R]   Usually done [U]   Unreliable [N]

At the present time, this pupil

copes well with this subject [CW]
copes adequately with this subject [CA]
copes adequately with a less academic
   approach to this subject [LA]
finds difficulty with this subject [FD]

Subject	Teacher	Group	Description of work	Homework	How she is coping	Appointment advised
English						
Mathematics						
Physics						
Chemistry						
Biology						
French						
German						
History						
Geography						

Table 1.4: continued

Subject	Teacher	Group	Description of work	Homework	How she is coping	Appointment advised
RE						
Textiles						
Art						
Home Economics						
Music						
PE						

Signed _____ Form Teacher [   ]

Chapter Two

GETTING STARTED

By Christmas 1986, members of the working party had investigated ways of encouraging First Year pupils to record their achievements so far. In mathematics for instance, a page was used at the end of their exercise books and headed either 'An Evaluation of My Work' or more pragmatically, 'My Achievements'. The evaluation took the form of incomplete sentences which, after class discussion to ensure meanings were understood, the pupils were asked to fill in. The sentences included,

     I am pleased with these achievements; ...
     I think the booklets are ...
     I feel that ...
     I think ...
     During the next few weeks I ...

The children were able to focus their attention on what they had been doing in lessons, and they provided their teachers with a useful insight into their thoughts and feelings. It was the kind of feedback which teachers have not been used to receiving because many of them have not asked for children's comments before. One of the problems in asking for comments is that one has to accept all comments with a good grace, whether they are complimentary or not; they are after all the children's perception of what has been going on. Obviously it would not be very reassuring for the teacher to discover that some of the children find her lessons difficult to understand, or that the homework takes too long, or that she cannot be heard from the back of the room, or that the work is too easy, and so on, but if it seems, on careful evaluation of the evidence, to be the case, then a change in approach is probably called for.

The following are some examples of the mathematics comments.

I am pleased with these achievements:

Pupil 1   I have been successful in statistics. The booklets are things which I have never done before, and they are a lot of fun.

Pupil 2   I feel I have achieved something in 'Number Machines' - it is new to me and it is completely different to any other maths that I have done. I think also this maths book makes it fun at the same time as work - I mean such as the games in the book.

Pupil 3   I am pleased I have got many of them right. They seemed hard, but I found I could do them.

In response to the statement 'I think the booklets are ...', they wrote,

Pupil 1   I think the booklets are enjoyable, interesting and helpful.

Pupil 2   I think the booklets are quite helpful, very different from the things I did at my other school.

Pupil 3   I think the booklets are good - parts are hard and parts easy. Some of the words are a little difficult to read, but I have worked them out.

The sentence beginning with 'I feel ...' was completed as follows:

Pupil 1   I feel I am doing quite well in maths. I feel quite confident that I might be able to finish all the booklets by the end of the year. (She did finish Level 1 by the summer).

Pupil 2   I feel maths lessons are enjoyable, interesting and helpful.

Pupil 3   I feel my maths is getting a bit better (like in questions on magnifying).

And finally, in their hopes for the future, they wrote:

Pupil 1   During the next few weeks I hope I shall make my work neater.

Pupil 2   During the next few weeks I shall try not to talk so much and learn some new things.

Pupil 3   I hope in future to work more neatly by underlining in pencil, ruling off in pencil, and not putting circles round the numbers of the question. (There was some helpful teacher intervention here!)

These comments were taken at random from the evaluation exercise of a mixed ability class and seem to me to show that these particular children were happy with their work and were gaining from it. The fact that they were able to identify targets to achieve in future was useful and supports the view that they were thinking about how they work. They were able to do the evaluation within two lessons, (allowing for initial explanations); the teacher took away their books to read, and returned them, commenting briefly and quietly to each child as she did so. She did not correct the grammar or spelling, neither did she write on them. This was a communication from the child to the teacher, and it would have seemed inappropriate to have 'corrected' it.

Most of the members of the working party group made up a similar evaluation, tried it out with their classes and brought the results back to the group for discussion. This sharing of what we had done represented an important step forward in the group's cohesiveness. In some cases in particular, it had required a lot of courage to try this approach with children, as the first few times it is done seem like large steps into the unknown. It needs the teacher to be confident that, even if the outcome is not as complimentary as she might have liked, she will be able to look at it with an open mind and try to alter things accordingly. In fact, most evaluations, if constructed carefully, will reveal some good things even if these might be overshadowed by whatever needs changing. It goes some way towards the research based model of teaching advocated by L. Stenhouse in 1975, who linked classroom research with 'bettering classroom experience' and pointed to the need of teachers to increase the understanding of their work through looking critically at it. At the same time he concluded that a 'close examination of one's teaching in order to improve it is personally threatening ...' and that a

25

supportive atmosphere in schools was needed in helping to overcome this.

However, the evaluation which we are talking about here is not only to enable the teacher to change if necessary. There were other important objectives such as that the child should be able to review what she has learnt, to focus on the process of learning and on how she can learn more effectively in the future. It should give her the opportunity of putting things into the wider perspective of personal development as she considers not only what she thinks about her learning, but also, how she feels about it. And for both teacher and pupil, it offers the opportunity to exchange ideas on a more democratic level than maybe has been expected in the past. In giving the pupil the chance to say what she thinks, even if it has to be on paper, the teacher is saying that she wants to listen to what her pupils have to say. By doing so, she is showing interest in the pupils and valuing their comments. Most people respond well to communicating with others when they know they are being listened to, and children are no exception to this.

At this time of sharing ideas and experiences in the Working Party, we discovered that the English department had introduced a new system of evaluating children's work. This consisted of a comment on what had been written, and children were encouraged to respond to the teacher's comment with one of their own. In some cases a dialogue developed between the teacher and child. The idea of this development was so that the pupil would take note of the comment instead of being content just to see A B or C at the end of a piece of work. Even if a grade and a comment were given, it was the department's experience that the children were really only interested in the grade, whereas it was the comment which was considered to be more meaningful. The other difficulty which the department faced was how to encourage children who, if graded, would often find themselves with a low grade. Departmental policy is to encourage pupils in a mixed ability setting, and the teachers felt that a grade which calls attention to the differences between children's ability was unsatisfactory and unmotivating. With the new arrangements for marking, they were able to record the grade in their mark book, without having to discourage the child by announcing it in her book. They hoped that the dialogue they entered into would help the child to look at specific areas for improvement or praise.

Developments were also taking place in the school's pastoral system which saw an increase in participation in discussion between teacher and pupil through the active tutorial work sessions. Tutorial work had been embryonic in nature for the previous two years, but, regular after school meetings of tutors had started to facilitate the development of ideas and methodology, in a kind of on-going INSET. Form tutors were becoming more comfortable in encouraging group work and discussion during tutorial time and this led to an interest in discussing the progress reports individually or in groups with members of their forms. The second year tutors pioneered this idea, and it proved so successful, despite an acute lack of time, that the third year tutors asked for and were allowed an amount of timetabled time to discuss the progress reports in conjunction with the pupils' choices for options.

At first, the teachers were concerned both about the structure of the discussions and also their own skills of negotiation. Fortunately the school had planned an afternoon of INSET in tutorial work skills which happened to fall just before the discussions about the reports. The objectives for that afternoon were in line with the increasing move within the school to discuss the children's work with them, and these included:

to experience a range of active learning methods
to allow open discussion of feelings about and towards tutorial work
to identify and attempt to understand feelings of insecurity sometimes felt by teachers using unfamiliar methods
to identify, through experiential learning, feelings with which pupils may have to cope during tutorial work.

Various activities were organised by a group of four teachers who planned the afternoon so that everyone could participate. The activities were so structured that even the most apprehensive was able to look back at the end of the afternoon and wonder why she had been so concerned. The stress throughout was on teaching through active learning which is characterised by the teacher acting as facilitator; by the student being involved and participating; by accepting that feelings, and not just knowledge, form an important part of learning; by the open nature of the relationship between teacher and pupil in which the teacher

27

shows interest in the personal development of the student, and by the responsibility which the pupil is encouraged to take towards her own learning (see Brandes and Ginnis, 1986).

Active learning methods include games, role play, questionnaires, group discussion, self-evaluation, decision-making exercises, and paper and pencil exercises to trigger thought, or to sum up the activity. During the afternoon, we had time only to experience a few of these so we selected games, questionnaires, group discussion and role play as being particularly relevant to our stage of development. We hoped to show that a critical part of the learning process is to be found in the post-learning discussion - when the teacher's role is to help pupils to draw meaning from it and perhaps to generalise the learning into future situations. The purpose of the activity for the pupil is that she should have thought about the situation and considered and tried out responses; and that she should have experienced her own and other people's feelings in a supportive environment as a preparation for life outside the classroom.

This kind of INSET forms a useful background to the introduction of records of achievement in a school as it enables teachers to look at alternatives to the formal approach to learning. One afternoon, of course, is nothing like enough INSET to cater for the wide range of learning which can be experienced through using these methods, but at least it is an introduction. A very valuable way of developing ideas from here is through sharing classroom experiences. We have found this only happens in groups when teachers have some confidence that others will understand what they are trying to do; it does, of course, occur between teachers who work closely together, but groups have an advantage over friendship dyads in that they offer more opportunity for diversity of ideas and thought, often bringing together teachers with a wide variety of experience.

The first few weeks after our INSET was marked by a noticeable increase in cohesiveness in the tutors' meetings, and a willingness to suggest ideas and ways of working; and to share individual experiences, both those that had worked and those which did not work so well! Our Second Year Tutors tried out with their groups and then discussed the trust exercises they themselves had undertaken at the INSET. They made the point that the games were enjoyed by their tutor groups and did generate feelings of trust, but that they did not work in classrooms and that, at times, they produced a lot of noise. We decided as a result that it might be more appropriate for these games to take place in the hall or gymnasium, which could be scheduled for use at tutor time, as this would provide the group with far more space and alleviate the problem of the noise disturbing other groups.

From the records of achievement point of view, however, the most relevant INSET activity on the tutorial work skills afternoon was the role play. This was also the activity which had been most feared by participants, but in the event, it was the activity which was mentioned more often than any other in the evaluation as being the most enjoyable. The activity started with a simple example of role play: 'You bought some pyjamas a week or so ago. When they were washed, you discovered they had shrunk by six inches in the arms and legs. You decide to take them back. Role play your discussion with the assistant'.

After a few minutes, the activity was stopped, and participants were asked to talk to each other about how they felt in their role. How did anything which was said or done affect them? Did each feel happy with the outcome? They should now change roles and see how it feels to be the other half of the conversation, which they then discuss.

The main role play activity was as follows: There are two parts to be played, (A) the teacher - Mrs Coldshoulder and (b) the pupil - Alison. Each player only has one set of instructions, so they do not know what the other person is going to do or say.

A. THE TEACHER – MRS COLDSHOULDER

You are busy organising your papers and visual aids, preparatory to getting started on the lesson. The television is being a bit temperamental - and you were only just thanking your lucky stars that you had managed to get it into your room before someone else arrived, claiming they needed to use it. You said they could have it after you had shown your video - but your lesson depended on it. Alison arrives at your desk and asks a question. You have got other things on your mind right now, and if she had any sense, she could see that quite clearly.

B   THE PUPIL - ALISON

You have been thoroughly disgruntled since Mrs
Coldshoulder gave you a C+ for your project last week.
You've complained to your mother and your friends; even
your Nan had to hear all about it. After all, it just wasn't
fair. You'd done all that work, copied page upon page out of
the encyclopedia, added one or two bits of your own,
checked with everyone else that you had done about the
right number of pages, and what happens? C+. No 'Well
tried, Alison' or 'Lovely, Alison, I did like your information
on hippopotamuses' but just C+! Lisa got B+, and she copied
from the same book as you did. It's not fair. Mrs
Coldshoulder can't like you for some reason. So you
determine to find out why you got such a low mark. You
haven't much to lose - she can't change the C+ to D just
because you ask. She's only messing about with the
television now - that might be a good time to talk to her ...

Some minutes should be allowed for this to develop and
at an appropriate moment, stop the activity and ask the
participants to share with each other how they felt in role.
They could describe to the other person what they were
trying to do, and it would be interesting to see how well
they were thought to have succeeded. Would you change
anything you said, or would you alter your approach another
time? Did they understand the other person's point of view?
How did they feel about the outcome?

Once roles have been exchanged more general questions
could be explored, such as can they relate this situation to
others with which they have had to deal? What have they
learnt from the activity? This could lead to discussion on
assessing work, on grading it and on the teacher's
responsibility or otherwise for talking to the pupil about the
work and its grade.

The tutorial INSET helped teachers to feel a little more
comfortable in talking to members of their forms about
their progress reports, but as it was the first year this had
been attempted they were fairly apprehensive about it.
However, it could be seen as an extension of the teacher's
role in that many of them have talked to children about
their work in the past; this represented a more structured
discussion, with a distinct move towards listening to what
the pupil also had to say. This was quite difficult, as with

the pressure of time, there was a tendency to put words into the child's mouth which she did not have time to formulate in her mind. One of the staff said, 'It was very hard to hang back and wait until the girls had said what they wanted to say. I found I had to stop myself from saying things like - you do think such and such don't you? - instead of asking open questions, waiting for her to think through her reply. And also I had to stop myself from assuming that I knew what her answer was going to be. After all if I really did know what she was going to say, there wasn't much point in going through the charade of getting her to say it. In fact the girls did come out with things I hadn't expected - things which showed they were thinking about their work, and wanting to improve it. Sometimes I could help, if they said things like 'I want to work harder' by getting them to think of what they actually meant by that - such as being neater; reading more; concentrating harder in lessons; doing their homework away from the television, and so on.'

The pastoral developments, the discussions with pupils over their work, and the INSET afternoon were all taking place as the Working Party started to get to grips with their understanding of what records of achievement are. The principles on which recording achievement are based will now be discussed in the context of our First Year work, and it should be borne in mind that most of the working party were developing their ideas as they went along. We did not work from a model; our project, based on philosophical principles, came into existence as a result of our reading, thinking, looking at other people's ideas, discussions and trial and error.

RECORDS OF ACHIEVEMENT; WHAT ARE THEY?

Records of Achievement are essentially records which take into account 'a pupil's progress across the whole educational programme of the school, both in the classroom and outside, and possibly activities outside school as well' (DES, 1984). Sir Keith Joseph's initiatives present the view that personal records should contain only positive statements; that the record should be the property of the pupil and should be part of the learning process, whereby the pupil learns about herself, and begins to verbalise her capabilities. Profiles are usually drawn up as a structured base from which to select statements for the record of achievement, although it is possible for profiles to be completed in their own right, and also for records of achievement to be drawn up freely from the pupil's experience as she sees it at the time, rather than as a result of a prescriptive profiling document. A further essential feature of the record of achievement is that it should have been drawn up and discussed with the pupil whose record it is.

In our First Year project we referred to the record of achievement as the summative document, whilst the profiles were a part of the formative process. The summative document was the 'end product' and thus represented the final draft on the thinking, planning, assessing, talking, reviewing, and listening to other people's opinions which teachers and pupils had engaged in since Christmas 1986. This summative document replaced our traditional report - for First Year pupils only - at the end of the summer term, and included subject-specific skills, cross-curricular skills, social and personal qualities and skills, and achievements from outside the classroom. The extra-curricular achievements could be chosen from a range of activities engaged in at school, for instance, taking part in the musical production, learning to swim a width, being in a house or school team and so on, and there was opportunity also for achievements outside the school to be recognised.

We foresaw problems with recording achievements outside school. We were concerned lest children should think the school was 'prying' into what they do in their spare time, and there are some who would much prefer to keep the two areas of their lives separate. On the other hand we felt the opportunity should be there for outside school activities to be celebrated - hobbies such as cultivating plants in the garden; cooking, fishing, etc. It is tempting to say that some children might do a lot which would be considered to be *worthwhile* out of school, but in saying that, we as teachers are superimposing our values of what *is* worthwhile onto them and in true empiricist tradition, we would want to avoid doing this.

There is a further problem associated with the outside school activities and that is that much which is thought of as being an 'achievement' could be said to depend on parents who have encouraged and promoted activities such as playing the piano, going to dancing classes, going to gymnastics/swimming/athletics clubs and so on. Of course this is fine for those families for whom it happens, but what about the others, where the emphasis is on different things and clubs and classes do not hold an appeal? Are we, by recording these out of school achievements, covertly valuing what parents have been doing for their children, and does this not defeat to an extent the purpose of the enterprise?

There are other activities which could be claimed as achievements, for instance visiting elderly people, shopping for the housebound, helping mum or dad regularly and willingly. But do children and their parents look on these activities as achievements, or is it taken for granted that they should be done or not as the case may be and therefore not worthy of further mention? Furthermore, by discussing these activities with our pupils, might we be encouraging them to want to do these things and thus bring them into conflict with their parents who, for very good reasons such as not wanting them out after dark, might not want to give them permission?

The summative document - the record of achievement - was intended to be a description of the pupil and was a skills based document. It gave the parent a detailed account of what the child could do in relation to the work she had been following throughout the year (Table 2.1 shows part of a completed document for one pupil). It also recorded some of her attitudes towards herself, her friends and towards studying and it gave an account of what she had been doing outside the classroom. It was mainly criterion referenced and only at times did it compare her with other members of her class. This was in relation to examination results where her result was juxtaposed with the year average; thus parents were able to see that as regards a particular result, their daughter was above, below or on the average for the year.

Records of achievement are based on evidence. Part of the subject-specific profiles, which made up the formative process, consisted of skills and levels of attainment (see Table 2.2 - textiles skills as an example). Departments were expected, as far as possible, to come to a common understanding of each level of the skills which they had identified, and these should have been based on the evidence of a child's exercise book, or on test marks or as a result of reflecting back over working behaviour during the year. The decisions arrived at as a result of looking at the evidence were then open to negotiation - or discussion; so that either the teacher or the pupil would need to revise her opinion if there was initial disagreement over the stated level of attainment which was thought to have been achieved. In practice, this was one of the most difficult parts of the process, particularly because of the time factor in 'negotiating' with 30/31 children over a range of skills.

PRACTICAL PROFILING; FOR WHAT PURPOSES?

Our profiles fed into the Records of Achievement and provided the documentation for the formative process, and it is particularly in the process of recording achievement that the benefits are seen to lie. Profiling means that the pupil will look back over her learning and think about it; she is then able to record what she feels she has achieved. In doing so, she has relinquished the passive role of having knowledge poured into her and is becoming more involved in her own learning. By becoming involved, she begins to take responsibility for her learning, and to own it as hers. As Brandes and Ginnis (op.cit.) have shown,

> ... the term ownership refers not just to the legal and moral right of possession, but to the *motivation for care, maintenance and development* of that which is owned.
>
> Possession + responsibility = ownership
>
> To own something, to us, means to take full responsibility for it. (Emphasis mine).

Thus ownership of learning induces motivation of pupils, and through motivation, an interest in setting targets for improvements - in deciding how she can change her learning behaviour for the future.

The process of profiling is seen as advantageous also because it shows that the teacher is interested in the child's progress. It is a development of the kind of relationship between teachers and pupils which has been mentioned elsewhere in this book; it implies that the teacher is going to listen to the child - but more than that, it has to imply that the teacher will listen to and respect what the child has to say. She may not agree with what is said, but if she does not, then, as in any conversation, she will find a way of saying so which does not destroy the burgeoning self confidence of her pupil. John Holt (1964) has said that 'it is a rare child who, anywhere in his growing up, meets even one older person with whom he can talk openly about what most interests him, concerns him, worries him'. If this is the case, it is to be hoped that the movement towards developing profiling in schools will provide the pupils with a much needed opportunity for discussion which has the potential to be both open and non-judgemental.

Profiling can improve the quality of reporting to parents in two respects. Firstly, profiles rely less on the teacher's subjective value judgements, and secondly, the system of reporting is fairer, because it has been talked about, negotiated, and hopefully, understood.

Comments based on profiles have lost that subjective quality which so characterised reports in the past. Not only did reports suffer from the syndrome of the passive, tidy, hard working child who received a good report which may merely have been based on the fact that she was no trouble, but also, reports were notoriously likely to reflect the most recent altercation with a pupil if she were given to upsetting the teacher. And after all, what did 'satisfactory' or 'could do better' actually mean to anyone, apart from being a useful butt of the comedian's humour against the teacher? Furthermore, comments made by teachers have traditionally been believed by parents, yet they are only opinions, and opinions at best based on only a brief acquaintanceship, shared between twenty nine or thirty others. Who is likely to know best whether the child spends her time daydreaming - the teacher or the child? A teacher's subjective judgement takes responsibility for behaviour away from the child, so she has no obligation to improve, whereas a negotiated profile goes some way towards involving the child in seeing the relevance to her progress of her behaviour. She can then decide, if she will, to do something about it - but the responsibility for doing so is hers, and not the teacher's.

PROFILES: SOME OF THE PROBLEMS

By the time the Working Party had thought through the philosophy of profiling, the nature and extent of the potential problems in implementing profiling/records of achievement had become clearer. There were three issues which assumed monumental importance, of which two would be far more difficult to deal with than the third. In order of degree of difficulty they were: (1) availability of time for planning the profiles and for operating the system (e.g. negotiating with the pupils); (2) necessity of providing sufficient supportive INSET and (3) resources needed for files, paper and storage facilities.

The reader will probably recognise that (3) above - the resources needed - is a practical problem which, given goodwill and interest on the part of a Head Teacher, can usually be resolved, albeit complaints about the paper-intensive nature of the exercise are bound to occur. Compared to the other two problems, however, it stands out as being amenable to relatively simplistic solutions. The problems of time available and of INSET required are worrying; of the two, it is possible to organise INSET if there is time available, so we are left with the time factor as the major obstacle to be overcome if the school really wants a profiling/records of achievement system.

These issues will be considered in the following chapters, but it is worth saying here that the only way the time problem will come nearer to resolution, is if teachers recognise that profiling is an integral part of the work children do in their lessons; it is part of their personal development and is valid in its own right. If profiling is seen as an optional extra; as a new idea for reports; or as a purely cognitive exercise to check up how much the children have learnt, then the non-availability of time will kill off any such project which was evidently built on a misunderstanding of the principles involved. It should be remembered throughout that, although profiling has to be based on a system, and the system might seem complex, it is the process of profiling - the thinking and understanding, the involvement in learning, the teacher/pupil relationships - which is of considerable educational value and, as such, integral to the learning experience.

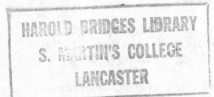

Table 2.1: Part of a Record of Achievement

Sally Whitehall   1H

Sally has discussed her year's work with her teachers and the following is a record of some of her skills and achievements at the present time.

English
When using her imagination to write stories and poems, she has lots of ideas which she can write about confidently. She can write down her ideas carefully, paying attention to spelling and punctuation rules. Sally knows quite a lot of words, and can use her dictionary to help find those that she does not know. In her own reading she can choose a book and can read it to herself. She can read clearly and with expression to the class. In discussion or drama lessons, Sally takes part and enjoys expressing her ideas to other people.

Mathematics
When Sally is using the four rules of number, she works accurately and she can use these skills to work out most problems on her own. Sally can remember most of the mathematical ideas covered during the year and can follow written or spoken instructions on her own. She usually presents her work in an orderly way. Sally mostly makes good use of time in lessons. Her aural test was 95%. Her examination result was 97% and the examination average for the year group was 66%.

Science
Sally can usually follow instructions by herself and when working in the laboratory, she follows the safety rules carefully at all times. When looking at living things, pictures and diagrams, she usually notices a few things of importance about them. Sally can think of lots of ideas and finds some of her solutions to problems work well. Sally can write an account of her science work accurately and with clear explanations. Her test result was 72% and the test average for the year group was 61%.

Table 2.1: continued

French

When listening to simple French being spoken, Sally can understand most of it. She can manage simple 'er' verbs and can always understand the French passages she reads. Sally can describe the weather and seasons in French well and can make herself understood, using the verb correctly, when writing French. Her examination result was 85% and the average for the year was 62%.

Table 2.2: Textiles Skills

Date_____ 19____

Teacher_____ Name_____ Form_____

	pupil's opinion	teacher's opinion
MANAGING THE MACHINE When setting up the machine		
T1 I can do this with help		
T2 I can manage this on my own		
When using the machine		
T3 I can machine if given some help		
T4 I can machine accurately		
T5 I can dial a pattern and machine accurately and confidently		
MANIPULATIVE SKILLS When handsewing, -tacking, and some embroidery stitches		
T6 I can work a few different stitches if someone shows me the method		
T7 I can work some different stitches fairly neatly		
T8 I can work several stitches accurately		
T9 I can work a variety of stitches neatly and accurately		
DESIGN SKILLS When we make up designs using colour and shape		
T10 I can make a simple design if someone helps me		
T11 I can make up a design on my own		
T12 I can make an attractive design and suggest ideas for stitches		
T13 I can make up attractive, detailed designs on my own		

Chapter Three

THE PROFILES - HOW THEY CAME ABOUT

In this chapter, I intend to show some examples of the profiles which we drew up for the summer of 1987. It is important to note that these were for our First Year pupils and it is extremely unlikely that, as they stand, they would be applicable to any other school, for reasons which will become apparent soon. The system we operated consisted of subject-specific profiles and personal and social skills profiles which all fed into summative documents. These summative documents were to be the First Year Record of Achievement. As things turned out, however, part of this process was computerised, so that the end product was different in appearance, but not in principle, from that which we had originally projected.

It will probably assist understanding of what we did, if we use an example at this stage for discussion purposes. Tables 3.1 and 3.2 show the two pages of the home economics profile. Six skills have been chosen for assessment, and for most of them, three levels of attainment are shown. There is space for the pupil's opinion of her work, and also for the teacher's opinion. The last part of the profile provides a more open opportunity for the pupil to comment - in particular this gives her the chance to note both what she has enjoyed, and also, in 'any other comments', what she might hope to do in the future. This was to be the target-setting part of the profile. The one norm-referenced item is concerned with the result of a specific test, namely the examination.

Table 3.3 shows what would have been the summative document from the home economics teacher. This was based entirely on the profile, which had been negotiated with the pupil. The skills were listed at the top of the page, and there is space for a more personalised series of comments below. If for instance, the pupil had achieved HE2 and HE5, the comment on the record of achievement would have read: 'At the present time this pupil can ... (kitchen management skill) ... usually think out what to do next and pick out the equipment she needs without help'.

One of the problems with this record is that it would be extremely time-consuming for each teacher to fill in for the 30 or so children in each of her classes (perhaps fewer in the example of home economics, but nevertheless for quite substantial numbers), so we put a high priority on trying to computerise the summative documents. Eventually a method was found by which we could use the computer to suit our purposes, so the subject teachers were spared from writing out the detailed record of achievement. This was fortuitous for all teachers, but particularly the RE department, one of whose staff took four of the five first year classes!

The system I have outlined of profile + record of achievement was standard for each subject and it was based on our belief in 'curriculum led' student profiling (see J. Mansell in P. Broadfoot's 'Profiles and Records of Achievement', 1986). Curriculum led profiling focuses on the curriculum and is to do with the skills, attitudes, concepts and knowledge which each subject wishes to assess in its pupils during the year. It is thus idiosyncratic both to the subject, the year group and obviously, also, to the school. It is for this reason that profiles developed in one school will not necessarily be transferable to another school, although the format and ideas might be open to more widespread use. It is also the case that from looking at another school's efforts in profiling to composing your own can seem a deceptively simple step to take. I should like to stress that designing, planning and wording profiles is not a simple exercise, and the more they are thought about, the harder it is to put into words what you want to say succinctly, unambiguously and in a way which is capable of being read and understood by all participants.

Before a profile is drawn up, the teacher needs to have sorted out the answers to some fundamental questions, such as 'what are we doing in our lessons, and why are we doing that in particular?' The work being done in class should be related to the aims and objectives for the lessons, and once the teacher has clarified in her mind what learning is or should be taking place, she is in a better position to see which skills and attitudes are amenable to assessment. Assessment can be used for two purposes; it can be used to evaluate courses, making adjustments where necessary, and it can also be used to determine where the pupil 'is now', and what the most appropriate learning strategies are for her future development.

J. Mansell (op. cit.) has explained that

by assessment, we mean generally a recorded judgement resulting from any testing situation, from a personal subjective observation, or from any mix of these. The testing situation may range from well-validated objective tests, scored by using an interval scale of measurement, through problem and essay type tests, assignments, etc, scored on less statistically advanced scales, to judgements based on observation, dialogue or interrogation, scored impressionalistically, some by the students themselves.

The skills identified on our profiles were assessed through a mixture of tests and subjective judgement; objective tests, however, were not included in our assessment procedures. Assessment was carried out by the teacher, by the pupil herself, by discussion with peer groups, and by negotiation between teacher and pupil.

Departmental skills were identified through departments looking at the range of work covered in the first year, and at the aims and objectives for the teaching. They then decided which of the skills they taught they wished to assess and record. This introduced us to a practical problem, which was that some departments wanted to assess far more skills than it was realistic for them to do. They felt that their First Year course was heavily based on skills, and that it would be invidious to put in some skills at the expense of others.

This was a particular problem for the PE department, and really centred on whether the profile should contain each skill taught, or whether it was acceptable to take an overview of the work covered during the year. The reader will see from Tables 3.4, 3.5 and 3.6 that the PE profiles are quite extensive in terms of covering a wide range of the syllabus, but as regards individual skills subsumed under the umbrella of, for instance, 'gymnastics', such as 'headstand with bent legs'; 'headstand with straight legs'; 'handstand to forward roll'; 'handspring', 'cartwheel', etc., there is a seemingly endless list of skills which individual children could achieve, and which we have not listed.

We felt we had to take into account, at this stage, the aims of our project, and the relevant one was that the profile should feed the summative document. The PE department, by virtue of the practical nature of their lessons, had difficulty in allocating time for profiling. Had the profile been extensive, the time problem would have been exacerbated, and the protracted negotiation which might have taken place in discussing whether Mary (and 29 others) could do a straight legged handstand or only the bent legged variety would simply have been totally unmanageable. As it is, therefore, the profile was generalised in the interests of sanity, though not necessarily in keeping with the highest expectations of profiling philosophy!

It could be that the answer to the problem lies in a preliminary, continuous profile, integral to the gymnastics/dance/swimming courses. Maybe 'negotiation' of the individual skills could take the form of brief teacher/pupil discussion during practical sessions, and the skills could be added to the profile routinely when achieved. From time to time, the more general profile which supports the record of achievement, could be considered.

There is a danger, however, of developing a checklist mentality, where the only things which come to be valued are the skills on the list. The corollary to this is that if the list is restrictive then the teaching will be also; that in PE it might be comparatively easy, given time (which is scarce), to assess physical skills, but much else of a creative and cooperative nature is also happening which is a lot more difficult to assess, and may, therefore, be pushed into the background. It should be remembered that the *curriculum* should lead the assessment rather than that the *assessment procedures* should dominate the curriculum, and that what we are aiming for is that the pupil will be in a position of standing back to look at her personal development, of which in PE lessons, the physical skills form a part, but not the whole.

To an exent, Geography and Religious Education had a similar problem of finding it difficult to condense their list of skills to be manageable and still to say what the teachers thought was important in covering the skills on their First Year syllabus (see Tables 3.7 to 3.11). The other problem which is tied in with this for these departments (and some others) is that with only one or two lessons a week, the prospect of negotiating some seven or eight skills with 30 children individually, is a daunting one.

DECIDING ON COMMENT BANKS

Having established the relevant skills, the next stage is to work out comment banks or statements which will define the level of attainment of the pupil. This is far easier said than done, for reasons which will become clear during the following discussion.

The principles which guided our thinking were that:

(1) the comments should be able to be read by 11 to 12 year old pupils;
(2) they should be easy to understand;
(3) they should be unambiguous;
(4) they should reliably describe what the child can do in relation to a particular skill;
(5) they should show a differentiation between levels of attainment;
(6) they should be limited in number;
(7) they should be transferable to the summative document.

These principles did guide our thinking, but, from time to time, we found ourselves losing sight of them, as we struggled to reach a consensus on what we wanted to say, and to convey that meaning unequivocally to all the participants of our scheme.

We found that words mean different things to different people, and that groups of words are even more prone to this condition. The fact that a few of our pupils function at a fairly low level of reading and understanding compounded the problem, making simplicity an essential component of our efforts. This limited our choice of words and made it difficult to avoid a repetitious use of words like 'usually', 'always', 'with help', 'with guidance'.

We might have liked to describe some of the skills themselves in more specific language, but to have used, for instance, 'chronological skills' or 'empathetic skills' in history, would have been to deny the importance of the children for whom the profiles have been drawn up in the first place. They had to be in a language which most of the children could understand without problems, and so we overcame this difficulty in two ways. Firstly, we tried to give a title to a skill which was phrased in everyday terms, and secondly, we then went on to describe the activity in a simple, incomplete sentence. This incomplete sentence put the skill in a personal context for the child, thus avoiding the generality of some of the titles. The history skills (Tables 3.12 and 3.13) are good examples of this:

(chronology) <u>Placing events in time order</u>
When we have to remember events in history in the order in which they happened ...
(empathy) <u>Imagining what it was like to live in Anglo Saxon times</u>
When I think about what it felt like to be an Anglo Saxon ...

The next part of the process was to differentiate between levels of skill attainment. This was a critical aspect of the profile, as, if different levels were not clear, or if they were not attainable, they would not be appropriate to the task for which they were designed. It was intended that, for the most part, they should be hierarchically organised, but when put into practice, teachers found that some levels of skill had been misappropriated. For instance, to use a further example from History, some pupils could use picture sources to find things out (H9), without really understanding why we need evidence to find out about the past (H8). It is clear from this example that the departmental evaluation of how well their profiles fitted what they wanted to assess will be an important part of the process for the teachers; it also points to the need to focus on clarity of aims and objectives in teaching and assessment and it is to the credit of many departments that they are reviewing their First Year work with this in mind.

Decisions had to be taken on the number of differentiated levels each department wished to use, and we found that it varied with the skill under consideration. On the whole, it was felt that three levels would be a manageable number for the teacher and pupil to cope with, but, as we experienced with the progress report, there was much discussion about whether the comments were differentiated appropriately, with some teachers feeling that more categories would better accommodate the range of attainment or behaviours within their groups. In particular, they felt that having only three categories ran the risk of putting most pupils in the middle, with only a few at either extreme. Four levels of achievement might have refined the decision-making, but to have been acceptable across a wide range of subject-specific skills, the assessment procedures would probably have needed to be more precise, and there would have been implications for negotiation as well. For a first-time profile, the three levels satisfied most people, but there is scope to develop these to more, if wished, as we become more experienced.

In History, where the department *has* used four levels in 'Placing events in time order' and five levels in 'Using evidence', it has used each level as a development of the previous one (see Table 3.12 and 3.13). For instance, using as a base 'the timeline', the simplest level of operation would be the personal one (concrete operations - Piaget). This moves upwards through the Anglo Saxons - one discrete group of people - and more generalised unspecified historical events, to the more abstract concept of AD and BC. This was a slightly different approach from most departmental profiles, although English and Textiles were, to an extent, similar. Most departments tended to use levels to evaluate in the sense of how well, or how often or how much or how much help was needed; for instance, Table 3.13 (History again, but also found in RE, Geography, Mathematics, etc.) shows in 'Remembering facts' that the pupil can remember 'some', 'quite a few' or 'a lot' of the things she has learnt. It was up to the departments to decide how these levels would be differentiated.

Some departments found that they preferred to use fewer levels in the sense that they thought for some of their skills either the pupil could do whatever was required or that she could not do it. For instance, in Home Economics, (Table 3.1), although three categories were felt to be right for organising oneself in the kitchen, it was thought that the pupils either could manage to choose and use the equipment without having someone to tell them what to do, or that they usually did need some advice, but that a third level of differentiation would have been unnecessary. On the same profile, however, in 'use of time', four sections have been identified, although in this case, these are not intended to be hierarchical. 'I need a lot of times to do things' (HE9) is not meant to imply any value judgement on that statement - some people do need to take time over things and this should be recognised. The other three statements do represent a progression from wasting time, to getting on regardless of everyone else.

POSITIVE STATEMENTS

This was the area which caused us the most concern and the most difficulty in resolving the problem.

By early March, much time had been spent in the discussion of skills, differentiated levels and the use of words to describe these, and we felt that most of the planning had been completed. It was only gradually, however, that we came to an awareness of the plight of the low achieving child. If a child were only achieving the lowest level in each skill, and there may be such children, then she would be going to take home a frightening record of what she could not do, or what she finds it hard to do. The lowest level of skill was usually phrased in terms such as 'finds it difficult to do ...' or 'finds it hard to ...' or 'I often make mistakes because ...'.

For instance, these examples are taken from a selection of different profiles:-

When we have to use our imagination to write stories and poems ... I find it hard to think of ideas.
When we are reading or talking in class ... I find some work is hard, because there are lots of words I don't know.
When we have to think of ideas ... I find it hard to think of anything.
When we write about our work ... There are often mistakes in my spelling and punctuation.
When we look at maps ... I need help to find things.
When we describe places, using geographical words ... I find it hard to use the right word.

And so on; there were examples in many of the profiles at this stage in their development.

It is interesting to remember that we had thought the comments were being stated quite positively, because we felt that, even though a child found mastery of the skill impossible, at least she had made an attempt at it, and with

47

help had achieved something. However, when each subject profile was complete, the cumulative effect of ten or so subjects all saying that Janice found the work hard and needed help with everything, would be more than enough to damage her self-confidence. An important aim of the profiling process is to be found in the development of self-esteem through the recognition and celebration of achievement, and yet we seemed to be saying that some children had achieved very little to celebrate during the year. This was extremely worrying, and had implications concerning our expectations of some of our pupils which had never seemed as clear as they did then.

Some of our pupils did have special educational needs, and the awesome question was, that if they found so much difficulty in achieving the lowest level of many of the skills which they had been taught during the year, were we making life too hard for them? Had we taken adequate account of their special needs in our curriculum? Or was it a case of teachers setting the lowest level in the profile too high? And if so, how could we alter it to make the lowest level meaningful?

There was also a strong body of feeling which said, if the child cannot do whatever it is, surely we should say so! This was a very difficult point of view with which to deal, as it seemed professionally unsound to be wrapping up unsavoury 'facts' as we saw them, in any other way. The question really was though, were they 'facts' or could they be more accurately described as 'reality constructed as a result of teacher expectation'? If this were the case, were the teacher's expectations based on what she thought children *should* be able to do, rather than what their various abilities and efforts enabled them to do? By this stage we had moved into the complex theoretical arena of assessing students.

We went back to the principles of recording achievement. A record of achievement is a record of what a child can do; it is not a record of what she cannot do, or what she finds hard to do, or even what she makes a lot of mistakes whilst doing. The record of achievement should 'reliably describe what the child can do in relation to a particular skill', and in our case, the profile should feed into the summative document. Maybe if we were not applying that particular stipulation, then the situation might have been different, as our profile could perhaps have included negative comments. But, for this project, this was one of the guiding principles, and we therefore had to stick to it or start all over again, basing our work on different criteria. So we had arrived at a critical point, which would make or break the work we had done so far.

We decided to look at the skills again, and at what a low attaining child could actually achieve. We had to discover if the answer was - nothing - and we found, of course, that this was not the case. The question which was asked was, 'did these children sit in lessons and do nothing, or were they achieving something, even if it was not at a particularly high level of attainment?' And when the answer came back that they were doing something, the follow up which enabled us to proceed was, 'then what can she do in relation to each particular skill?'

When departments come to evaluating the process of recording achievement, they will not be able to dissociate an evaluation of their curriculum as it is offered to First Year pupils from the evaluation of the profiling process, and it may be that the experience of agonising over 'positive statements' will have served well the interests of future First Year pupils, especially those who do have special educational needs. We have a particular responsibility to ensure that we are attempting to meet those needs in the curriculum, within the constraints of staffing and resources generally. As we have seen from our experience and from the literature, the process of recording achievement sharpens the teacher's perceptions of the aims and objectives of her teaching, and renders awareness of assessment, and precision in assessment techniques an increasingly important part of her work. All this should lead to the ongoing development of the curriculum, to the advantage of all pupils.

And so, when we look again at the skills which we had found difficult to phrase in positive terms, we can see the tremendous improvement in the final documents. In Geography for instance,

> When we look at ordnance survey maps ... I can find things if someone helps me - thereby stressing what the child can do, and,
> When we describe places, using geographical words ... I can describe places using my own words.

In Science (Tables 3.14, 3.15)

> When we have to think of a few ideas ... I can usually
> think of one or two ideas, and
> When we write about our science work ... I can usually
> write accounts if someone helps me.

And in English (Tables 3.16, 3.17)

> When we have to use our imagination to write stories
> and poems ... I have one or two ideas, and
> When we are reading or talking in class ... I know and
> can undertand words which we come across often.

Although the words are only a little different, the emphasis
is totally changed in that the statements say what a child
can do, instead of what she finds difficult to do. Such has
been the movement forwards through a lot of troubled
thinking which eventually gave way to the reformed
versions, that departments would probably be reluctant to
own the previous comments as theirs, and I think they would
agree that overcoming this problem has been a very
significant step in our developmental progress.

CROSS-CURRICULAR SKILLS

Until the time that we began to identify departmental skills,
we had not fully appreciated the range and importance of
the cross-curricular skills. SERA - The South East Records
of Achievement - a pilot scheme in which Bexley, Kingston,
Merton, Surrey, Sutton and the South East Regional
Examinations Board are working together, has identified
eight general skills which would form part of the school
leaver's summative document. These are: information
handling; organisational; problem-solving; communication;
creative and imaginative; physical/motor; numerical; and
social skills.

Some of our school working party looked at cross-
curricular skills, and decided to concentrate on
communication, information handling and organisational
skills. These were the skills we felt that, at First Year level,
teachers and pupils could cope with, and they incorporated
attitudes, such as towards using time, presenting work,
contributing to discussions that we wished to encourage. Our
original attempt at 'communication' skills included reading
and understanding; oral; writing; and language skills; whilst

the 'information handling' skills consisted of presentation of work, remembering information, and following instructions. Use of time fell into the 'organisational' category.

When we originally looked at the SERA list of cross-curricular skills, some of them seemed too sophisticated for what we needed, and we thought they might have presented problems over how we were to assess them. 'Creative and imaginative' skills was one area which we felt might be difficult to work with. In the event, however, several departments - English, Science, Art, Pottery specifically, and textiles, music and PE by implication - identified this as a skill that they did wish to assess; art and pottery both following up the use of imagination by putting the ideas to work in practical situations, through 'when we make things from our ideas ...'. In English, using imagination was linked to writing stories and poems, in science it was followed by finding solutions to problems, and in other subjects it was linked to creating patterns, music and dances.

Several departments wanted to make use of the cross-curricular skills - information handling and organisation - detailed in Table 3.18, and we thought briefly about issuing it as an adjunct to their own subject-specific skills, but dismissed this idea as lengthening the process of assessment and negotiation beyond what was reasonable to expect. What eventually happened was that departments cut out one or two of their own skills and replaced them with a selection from the cross-curricular skills, as you can see in Table 3.19.

From our point of view, our brief was to produce a record of achievement which would replace the traditional report at the end of the summer term, so we felt we needed the stability of the subject-based approach. We had always been used to this and the school had not moved towards any real integration of subjects, but it was interesting to see the extent of general skills present and assessable across different areas of the curriculum. It gives rise to the future consideration of using a cross-curricular-based skills approach to the record of achievement, which would tie in well with the SERA project's summative document issued at the end of the Fifth Year to pilot school pupils only, at present. If we take science as an example, the science skills all fall within the general ones identified by the SERA Consortium:

general skills	science skills
information handling	following instructions
	working safely
	noticing things
creative and imaginative	having ideas
problem-solving	solving problems
communication	writing accounts

Looking at other subjects, it is clear that the subject-specific skills identified could be subsumed under the general process skills mentioned, thus offering a rather different perspective on the learning which has taken place during the year. We would be seeing that similar skills are developed in different lessons, thus stressing the transferability of the process of learning across the curriculum, rather than stressing the individuality of subjects within it. This should mean that learning is experienced as being more readily applicable to different situations; that it is no longer compartmentalised, and for instance, that the skills learnt in reading maps, plans and grids in mathematics, are applicable to the skills the geography department wishes to nurture in using maps and plans to obtain or show information. To put this concept into operation would require some fairly radical rethinking; interdepartmental cooperation; and management and inservice support.

SOCIAL AND PERSONAL QUALITIES

This is the final section of the record of achievement to be described, but it was planned to take precedence over the subject-specific skills, by being the opening page of the summative document. By putting it first we hoped to stress the importance of the development of personal and social skills and qualities, comments about which are often added perfunctorily at the end of a traditional report. The qualities suggested for discussion by SERA with a view to inclusion are as follows:-

    attitude to study
    care/pride in appearance
    cooperation
    courtesy and politeness
    initiative

perseverance
relating to others/community awareness
reliability
response to discipline
self-confidence
tolerance

In looking at personal qualities, we are entering a sensitive and possibly contentious area. Naturally most people like to be well thought of, and can be very hurt if someone else ventures to suggest that they could do with changing the way they are, or by suggesting that they see the person differently from the way she sees herself. This can be very damaging to the self-esteem; it can also be unfair, as someone is making a judgement on another person on the basis of the small amount of time in which she has known her. T.S. Eliot has expressed the transient nature of our knowledge of other people in 'The Cocktail Party' (quoted in D. Rowntree, 1977).

We die to each other daily.
What we know of other people
Is only our memory of the moments
During which we knew them. And they have changed
    since then.

Not only is the time factor of significance, but so also are beliefs and value systems. For instance on the one hand, a tolerant person can be seen to give other people a chance to express an opinion; to be a comfortable friend, because she accepts people as they are; to allow people to do as they wish; to be calm in day to day affairs, and so on. But she could also be tolerant of other people manipulating her; boring her; putting her down; being unkind. She might be tolerant of wrong doing; she might be tolerant of bullies; she might never make a stand on any matter of principle. But presumably when we talk about tolerance as a personal quality, we take it to mean the 'good' aspects of it - the accepting, the encouraging of other people, the being calm. This implies that there is only one side to tolerance, and that is not altogether the case.

A similar argument could be used for cooperation. At first sight this seems to be perfectly straight forward; we like people to be cooperative. But could it be that they co-operate because they have not thought out an alternative position; or because it is the policy of least resistance; or because they are too frightened to do otherwise, or because they will be liked if they do cooperate? If cooperation is seen as doing as you are asked, then there may be times when, as in tolerance, the individual should be prepared to decline.

If children learn to be tolerant and to be cooperative in school, do they also learn that there can be times or situations when they should be independent, when they should stand by what they think to be right, when they should speak up for what they believe in?

It has been suggested that by valuing the qualities listed, the school is covertly operating a policy of social control through which it is hoped that children will learn to be polite, quiet, obedient, friendly, kind to others, hard working, and so on. No doubt these are excellent qualities to encourage, but, some of them sit uneasily beside showing initiative, displaying self confidence and taking risks. This dichotomy should be remembered in drawing up personal profiles and it is something of which participants should be aware as they use them.

It is almost axiomatic to say that if profiles are to record personal qualities, then the school not only must provide opportunities for pupils to develop and show such characteristics as reliability, initiative, perseverance, self-confidence, and community awareness, but also it must show through its own ethos, that it recognises and values these qualities.

M. Rutter, B. Maughan, P. Mortimore and J. Ouston (1979), in 'Fifteen Thousand Hours', showed that

> schools in which a high proportion of children held some kind of responsibility in the school system had better outcomes with respect to both pupil behaviour and examination success. This was evident in terms of the proportion of children who had been form captain ... and also in terms of the proportion who had taken some kind of active role in a school assembly or other meeting.

There is a section on our personal and social skills profile for children to write in the activities in which they have taken part during the year (Table 3.20). Reflection on the findings about pupil outcomes from M. Rutter's study would seem to lead us towards encouraging schools to seek to expand the opportunities for pupils to participate and show responsibility, not just as form captains or games captains, but also in school council meetings, helping with visitors at prospective parents' meetings, open evenings etc., ushering in the audience at concerts and plays, acting as stage hands in drama productions and so on, and to ensure that these activities are valued through, amongst other means, having them recorded on the personal profile. Not only do these provide an opportunity for pupils to have contributed to the school community but they also provide an excellent chance to develop some of the personal qualities that we have mentioned.

In addition, our profile gives the opportunity for the pupil to record achievements from out of school (Table 3.21), which are validated by the adult with whom or for whom the activity was carried out. These achievement slips should be written up as the occasion warrants during the year - for example skating certificates or guide badges gained; home responsibilities regularly undertaken; taking part in sponsored events and so on - and added to the pupil's record of achievement at school.

The final part of the profile concerned with personal and social qualities, concentrated on attitude to study, getting on with other people, and pride in appearance. I feel that the whole process of recording achievement needs to be strongly supported by an active programme of pastoral work, which seeks to open discussion on attitudes and values and in which trust is developed between the pupil and the form tutor, and also between the pupils themselves. Some of the skills involved in profiling, such as recognising achievement, talking about it, setting short and long-term goals, peer group assessment, and becoming active in the school community will be areas of interest for the form tutor and the group to explore together. The development of personal qualities is also integral to the pastoral programme, and in order for a pupil to understand and assess this aspect of her life, it is necessary for activities and discussions to have taken place around various themes in tutorial time.

One of our main tutorial themes for First Year pupils is on friendship - the qualities of a good friend, the behaviour of friends towards each other, and towards 'outsiders', feelings about friends, trust, loyalty, jealousy, conflict, and ending friendships. So it seemed appropriate for each pupil to make some form of assessment of herself as a friend (see

Table 3.22). Having completed this as a self-assessment exercise, the girls were asked to discuss it with one of their friends to see if they agreed, and to see if they could remember any incidents which would support these statements. The remaining section encouraged the pupils to think about ways in which they could be a better friend in the future. For the summative document, the pupils were asked to choose one or two statements which they felt described themselves most accurately and these were written out by the tutor on the first page (Table 3.23).

Attitudes towards studying have also featured in tutorial sessions, and many of the staff thought this was a particularly important part of the profile. In encouraging the pupils to think of the behaviours most conducive to working hard in class and at home, it was felt that they were given the chance to talk about how they respond, how they might respond instead, and how they might care to change their behaviour in future. Some children do have an unrealistic view of how quickly they settle down to work, how long they concentrate for, how disturbing their behaviour is to other people, and on the other side of the spectrum, they sometimes do devalue their own efforts, perhaps because they do not achieve 'top' marks. By putting 'attitude to study' on the profile, the children are given the opportunity to discuss the way in which they work, to review and value what is generally considered as good practice and perhaps to set targets for themselves as a result.

The last section in our personal qualities profile concerned 'pride in appearance', despite the potential for conflict which this introduces - such as whose opinion will be validating the statements - pupil's, teacher's, or parent's? It is a known fact that what constitutes 'smart' or 'tidy' for one set of people does not automatically do so for the other groups! Neither do teachers and parents seem to understand the rigid youth culture rules governing what is 'in' and what is quite definitely 'out'. Furthermore, 'pride in appearance', if taken to excess, could conflict with other areas of personal development which we are anxious to promote. For instance, obsession with appearance can lead to a concentration on superficialities and on features about a person which cannot be changed; it can lead to invidious comparisons and jealousies both about other people's looks, and also about the quality of their clothes and possessions.

However, we hoped to render our profile relatively harmless but at the same time, useful in developing practical attitudes mainly towards preparation of clothes for school - in other words the organisational aspects of pride in appearance rather than the value-laden ones. We also felt that much stress had been laid on school uniform during the year, so discussion on it would allow freedom to express feelings which might otherwise remain at the festering and grumbling stage. At least if complaints are voiced, then the other side of the argument can be reliably made, and even if no changes are made, reasons will have been given for the decisions to maintain the status quo. If reasons are seen to be sensible, and consistent, then this may have the effect of making the school's uniform expectations on the pupils more acceptable.

So these three personal qualities - getting on with other people, attitudes to study, and pride in appearance were all included in the summative document (Table 3.23), together with the activities in which the pupil has participated, and a record of her attendance and punctuality during the year. We hoped this would give a picture of the pupil as she has been in her first year, with her own comments about herself to complete the picture. This should set the scene for the rest of the record, which would be a mainly positive account of what she can do at the present time.

Table 3.1: Home Economics Skills

Date_____ 19____

Teacher_____ Name_____ Form_____

KITCHEN MANAGEMENT When we have to organise what to do in the kitchen	pupil's opinion	teacher's opinion
HE1 I often need to ask what to do next		
HE2 I can usually think out what to do next		
HE3 I find I cope confidently		

USING EQUIPMENT
I am able to pick out and use the
equipment I need in the kitchen

HE4 with guidance		
HE5 usually without help		

USING A COOKER
When using a cooker

HE6 I can do this, but prefer to have someone to help me		
HE7 I can usually manage on my own		
HE8 I feel confident to do this on my own		

USE OF TIME

HE9 I need a lot of time to do things		
HE10 I take a lot of time before settling to work		
HE11 I mostly make good use of time in lessons		
HE12 I have a strong sense of personal motivation		

Table 3.2: Home Economics continued

Name_____

	pupil's opinion	teacher's opinion
REMEMBERING FACTS		
HE13 I can remember a few of the things we have learnt		
HE14 I can remember some of the things we have learnt		
HE15 I can remember most of the things we have learnt		

FOLLOWING INSTRUCTIONS

When we have to follow written or spoken instructions

HE16 I can do this if given some help		
HE17 I can do this if given one or two reminders		
HE18 I can follow instructions without having to be reminded		

The pieces of work I enjoyed most this year were

....

....

Any other comments...

My test result was ....% and the test

average for the year group was ....%.

Signed...

Table 3.3: Report Form

Home Economics

Name _____

Form _____

HOME ECONOMICS SKILLS	At the present time, this pupil . . .
organising work in the kitchen	
using equipment	
using a cooker	
use of time	
remembering facts	
following instructions	

ACHIEVEMENTS IN HOME ECONOMICS

The pieces of work she enjoyed most were...
....

Any other comments..

Her examination result was..........%, and the examination average for the year group was..........%

Table 3.4: Physical Education Skills

Date_____ 19___

Teacher_____ Name_____

	pupil's opinion	teacher's opinion
GYMNASTICS SKILLS When we are working in the gym		
P1 I can do one or two activities		
P2 I can do several activities, especially if given some help		
P3 I can make up simple sequences well, using gymnastics skills		
P4 I can do at least one vault		
P5 I can do a wide range of skills and vaults in a controlled manner		
DANCE SKILLS When we make up dance sequences		
P6 I can make up dance sequences if someone helps me		
P7 I can usually make up a sequence on my own		
P8 I can work together with a partner to make up a dance which contains a variety of movements		
GAMES SKILLS Netball skills including throwing, catching, shooting, running, jumping, marking, dodging		
P9 I can do some of these, some of the time		
P10 I can often do these well		
P11 I can do these well and have played in the school team		

Table 3.4: continued

Rounders skills including throwing, catching, running, fielding, hitting the ball, bowling etc.	pupil's opinion	teacher's opinion
P12 I can do some of these, some of the time		
P13 I can often manage these well		
P14 I can manage these well and have played in the school team		

The Profiles

Table 3.5: Physical Education continued

Name_____

ATHLETICS		
This is a record of my best performances		teacher's signature
P15 100m		
P16 200m		
P17 800m		
P18 1500m		

P19 long jump		
P20 high jump		
P21 javelin		
P22 discus		
P23 shot putt		

SWIMMING	pupil's opinion	teacher's opinion
P24 I can swim a short distance using a float		
P25 I can swim about two widths		
P26 I can swim some distance/ in a fairly good style		
P27 I can swim at least 20 lengths non stop, using good style and a range of strokes		

63

Table 3.5: continued

> I have particularly enjoyed...
>
> ....
>
> Any other comments...
>
> ....
>
> *Signed*...

Table 3.6

Name_____

AWARDS GAINED IN PHYSICAL EDUCATION

BAGA AWARDS	4	3	2	1		
DATE						
SPORTS ACROBATICS AWARD	3	2	1			
DATE						
FIVE STAR AWARD	1	2	3	4	5	
DATE						
PERSONAL SURVIVAL	1	2				
DATE						
WATER SKILLS	1	2	3	4	5	6
DATE						
DISTANCE SWIMMING (Maximum Distance)						
DATE						

Table 3.7: Geography Skills

Date_____ 19___

Teacher_____ Name_____ Form_____

SHOWING GEOGRAPHICAL INFORMATION When we have to draw plans	pupil's opinion	teacher's opinion
G1 I can draw simple plans with help		
G2 I can usually draw plans to scale		
G3 I can draw plans and sketch maps accurately		

When we work with graphs and need to plot information

G4 I can do this if given help		
G5 I can usually manage to do this		
G6 I can do this and interpret information from the graph		

OBTAINING GEOGRAPHICAL INFORMATION
When we look at ordnance survey maps

G7 I can find things if someone helps me		
G8 I can usually find what we are looking for		
G9 I can read and get information from the map		

When we use atlases to recognise
continents, countries, seas, oceans,
rivers, mountains, deserts, etc.

G10 I can find a few of these		
G11 I can find these with only a little help		
G12 I can find these and use the key and index		

The Profiles

Table 3.8: Geography continued

Name_____

	pupil's opinion	teacher's opinion
WRITING ABOUT PLACES When we describe places, using geographical words		
G13 I can describe places using my own words		
G14 I can describe places using some geographical words correctly		
G15 I can use geographical words confidently		
PRESENTATION OF WORK		
G16 I find writing and drawing difficult to do neatly		
G17 I can do my writing and drawing neatly if I try hard		
G18 My work is usually neat		
REMEMBERING FACTS When we have to remember signs, symbols, geographical words, and other information		
G19 I can remember a few of the things we have learnt		
G20 I can remember some of the things we have learnt		
G21 I can remember most of the things we have learnt		
USING TIME		
G22 I need a lot of time to do things		
G23 I take a lot of time settling down to work		
G24 I mostly make good use of time in lessons		
G25 I have a strong sense of personal motivation		

Table 3.9: Geography continued

Name_____

The piece of work I most enjoyed doing this year was

....

Next year I should like to improve.............................

My examination result was ......% and the examination

average for the year group was ....%.

Signed...

Table 3.10: Religious Education Skills

Date_____ 19____

Teacher_____ Name_____ Form_____

	pupil's opinion	teacher's opinion
MAP WORK When we are asked to draw maps		
RE1 I can draw them with some help		
RE2 I can draw them with only a little help		
RE3 I can draw them on my own		
When we use maps to find places mentioned in the Bible		
RE4 I can find them if I have some help		
RE5 I can usually find them by myself		
MAKING THINGS e.g. POSTERS, MASKS etc. When we had to cut, paste, and put together what we needed for our ideas		
RE6 I know what I wanted my work to look like		
RE7 My work looked something like I wanted it to		
RE8 I managed this on my own		
PRESENTATION OF WORK		
RE9 I find it difficult to do my work neatly		
RE10 I can do my work neatly if I try hard		
RE11 I always manage to do my work neatly		

Table 3.11: Religious Education continued

Name_____

FINDING REFERENCES When we look for something in the Bible	pupil's opinion	teacher's opinion
RE12 I can find things if someone helps me		
RE13 I can manage with only a little help		
RE14 I can find it on my own		

REMEMBERING FACTS	pupil's opinion	teacher's opinion
RE15 I can remember some of the things we have learnt		
RE16 I can remember several of the things we have learnt		
RE17 I have a good memory for a wide range of facts		

DISCUSSION SKILLS When we're talking about things		
RE18 I know what I want to say, but don't always say it		
RE19 I usually take part and say what I think		
RE20 I always enjoy taking part and find it quite easy to express my ideas to other people		

USING TIME		
RE21 I need a lot of time to do things		
RE22 I take a lot of time before I settle to work		
RE23 I mostly make good use of time in lessons		
RE24 I get on with my work and do not waste time		

Table 3.12: History Skills

Date_____ 19____

Teacher_____ Name_____ Form_____

	pupil's opinion	teacher's opinion
PLACING EVENTS IN TIME ORDER When we have to remember events in history in the order in which they happened		
H1 I can draw a timeline of my life		
H2 I can draw a timeline for a few events for the Anglo Saxons		
H3 I can draw a timeline to show historical events		
H4 I can show the difference between AD and BC on a timeline		
IMAGINING WHAT IT WAS LIKE TO LIVE IN ANGLO SAXON TIMES When I think about what it felt like to be an Anglo Saxon		
H5 I can think of a few details about life in Anglo Saxon times		
H6 I can describe how the Anglo Saxons punished criminals, carried out trial by ordeal, buried their dead		
H7 I think I can understand how the Anglo Saxons felt about, e.g. punishment, trial by ordeal etc.		
USING EVIDENCE When we are using historical sources of evidence to find about the past		
H8 I understand why we need evidence		
H9 I can use picture sources to find things out		
H10 I can use written sources to find things out		
H11 I know what 'bias' means and that sources might be biased		
H12 I can usually tell the difference between primary and secondary sources		

Table 3.13: History continued

Name_____

REMEMBERING FACTS
When we are thinking about the Anglo
Saxons and their way of farming, their
ships, their religion, the Viking
attacks, etc

	pupil's opinion	teacher's opinion
H13 I can remember some things we have learnt		
H14 I can remember quite a few things about them		
H15 I can remember a lot about them		

PRESENTATION OF WORK

H16 I find it difficult to do my work neatly		
H17 I can do my work neatly (but sometimes I don't)		
H18 I always do my work neatly		

ACHIEVEMENTS IN HISTORY
I liked doing the work on...

....

I think my best pieces of work were............................

My aims for next year are...

My examination result was ....% and the examination

average for the year group was ....%.

Signed...

Table 3.14: Science Skills

Date_____ 19____

Teacher_____ Name_____ Form_____

	pupil's opinion	teacher's opinion
FOLLOWING INSTRUCTIONS When we are asked to follow instructions		
SC1 I can follow them but like to check that I am doing so correctly		
SC2 I can usually manage by myself		
SC3 I can follow instructions without the teacher's help		
WORKING SAFELY There are rules which help to make us safe when working in the laboratory		
SC4 I can follow the rules, but often need reminding of them		
SC5 I can follow them, but sometimes need reminding of them		
SC6 I follow the rules carefully at all times		
NOTICING THINGS When we look at living things, pictures and diagrams		
SC7 I usually notice one or two things		
SC8 I usually notice a few things		
SC9 I notice many things		
HAVING IDEAS When we have to think of ideas		
SC10 I can usually think of one or two ideas		
SC11 I can usually think of some ideas		
SC12 I can think of lots of ideas		

Table 3.15: Science continued

Name_____

SOLVING PROBLEMS When we are asked to solve a problem	pupil's opinion	teacher's opinion
SC13 I find a few of my solutions work well		
SC14 I find some of my solutions work well		
SC15 I find most of my solutions work well		

WRITING ACCOUNTS When we write about our science work		
SC16 I can write accounts if someone helps me		
SC17 I usually write accounts without help		
SC18 I often write accurate accounts and explanations		

The pieces of work I enjoyed most this year were

....

....

Any other comments...................................

My test result was ....% and the test

average for the year group was ....%.

Signed...

Table 3.16: English Skills

Date_____ 19____

Teacher_____ Name_____ Form_____

	pupil's opinion	teacher's opinion
WRITING SKILLS (1) When we have to use our imagination to write stories and poems		
N1 I have one or two ideas		
N2 I have lots of ideas, but it's not always easy to organise them without some help		
N3 I have lots of ideas which I can write about confidently		
WRITING SKILLS (2) When we are writing in class		
N4 I can write down some of my ideas		
N5 I can usually write down my ideas quite correctly		
N6 I can write my ideas carefully because I understand the rules of spelling and punctuation		
VOCABULARY SKILLS (knowing words and their meanings) When we are reading or talking in class		
N7 I know and can understand words which we come across often		
N8 I know quite a lot of words, and I can use my dictionary to help me find those I don't know		
N9 I know a wide variety of words, and I can use a dictionary or thesaurus to help improve my vocabulary		
LIBRARY/PERSONAL READING When we are reading to ourselves		
N10 I can choose a book (with guidance), and can read it to someone else		
N11 I can choose a book and read it to myself		
N12 I have read a wide range of books for pleasure or information		

Table 3.17: English continued

Name_____

	pupil's opinion	teacher's opinion
READING SKILLS When we read aloud in class		
N13 I can read aloud to a small group of friends		
N14 I can read aloud in class		
N15 I can read clearly and with expression to the class		
ORAL (TALKING) SKILLS When we're talking, discussing or doing drama work in English		
N16 I can say what I think to a friend		
N17 I can say what I think in a small group		
N18 I can take part in discussions and enjoy expressing my ideas to other people		

The piece of work I think I did especially well was.........

....

The hardest piece of work I had to do was...................

....

The things I have most enjoyed doing in English this

year have been...

....

Next year I would like to try to improve these parts of

my English work...

....

Signed...

Table 3.18: Cross-Curricular Skills

Name _____ Form _____ Date _____

Subject _____ Teacher _____

	pupil's opinion	teacher's opinion
PRESENTATION OF WORK		
A1 Finds written work difficult to do neatly		
A2 Can present work neatly if she tries hard		
A3 Frequently presents work clearly		
REMEMBERING FACTS		
A4 Finds difficulty in remembering basic facts		
A5 Can usually remember basic facts		
A6 Has a good memory for a wide range of facts		
FOLLOWING INSTRUCTIONS		
A7 Can follow simple written or spoken instructions if given some help		
A8 Needs only a little guidance to follow written or spoken instructions		
A9 Can follow written or spoken instructions independently		
USING TIME		
A10 Takes a lot of time before settling to work		
A11 Usually makes good use of time in lessons		
A12 Shows a strong sense of personal motivation		

Comments — if wished —

Signed by teacher and pupil..

Table 3.19: Cross-Curricular Skills continued

Name _____ Form _____ Date _____

CROSS CURRICULUAR SKILLS (Skills found in many different subjects)

	ENGLISH	MATHS	SCIENCE	BIOLOGY	FRENCH	EXT. ENGLISH	HISTORY	GEOGRAPHY	RE	ART	TEXTILES	HOME ECONOMICS	MUSIC	PE
Presentation of work														
Remembering facts														
Following instructions														
Using time														
Reading and understanding														
Oral skills														
Writing skills														
Language skills														

Table 3.20: Personal and Social Skills

Name _____

Date _____

I have been to school _____ times out of a maximum of _____ I have never been late/I have been late _____ times. I am pleased with my attendance and punctuality record/I think I should try to improve my attendance and/or punctuality record.

I have taken part in the following form or school activities:

an assembly on _____

house sports teams _____

school teams _____

raising money for _____

any other _____

Out of school, I have done/I belong to/I am responsible for/I look after/anything else I have a special interest in _____

_____

_____

_____

Please add record of achievement slip here, signed by an adult, describing what you have done.

Signed _____

Form teacher _____

Table 3.21: Out of School Activities

Name _____ Form _____ Date _____

I feel I have achieved something worthwhile in the following
activity

Signed............... Status............... Form teacher...............

I feel I have achieved something worthwhile in the following
activity

Signed............... Status............... Form teacher...............

80

Table 3.22: Attitude to Study

Date _____   Name _____

Ref.	Like me	Not like me		Especially in these lessons:
S1			I often talk about other things in class	
S2			I find myself daydreaming in lessons	
S3			Teachers often tell me to get on with my work	
S4			I can and do settle down to work quickly	
S5			I like to concentrate hard on my work	
S6			I think most teachers are pleased with the way I work	
S7			I am proud of a lot of my work	
TARGET SETTING:			In the next few weeks, I will try to	

Table 3.22: continued

GETTING ON WITH OTHER PEOPLE

Ref.	Like me	Not like me		Does my friend agree with me?
S8			I am usually friendly to people in my form	
S9			I share things with people	
S10			I listen to other people's worries and problems	
S11			I talk a lot	
S12			I try to notice how other people are feeling and help if I can	
S13			I have fallen out with several people this year	
S14			I find it hard to finish a friendship nicely	
S15			I do not talk about my friends behind their backs	
S16			Being with my friends makes me feel happy	
S17			I wish I had more friends	
TARGET SETTING:			I will try	

Table 3.22: continued

PRIDE IN APPEARANCE

Ref.	Like me	Not like me	
S18			I like to be tidy and smart for school
S19			I get my clothes ready the evening before
S20			I hope my mum or dad will clean my shoes
S21			I usually clean my shoes regularly
S22			I take my PE kit home at weekends to wash
S23			I often forget to take my PE kit home
S24			I sometimes forget to bring it back
S25			
S26			I always keep to the school uniform rules
TARGET SETTING:			I will try

Table 3.23: First Page of Record of Achievement

Name _____ Form _____ Date _____

This document is a record of your daughter's achievements during the previous year. Where possible, her teachers have discussed it with her, and she has also made contributions to it. We hope the document tells you significant features about her personal development, and would be pleased if you would return it for her to keep in school.

.... has attended school .... out of a possible .... up till .... 1987.
She has *always been on time/been late .... times.

.... has taken part in the following form or school activities:

assemblies on ....
house sports events ....
school teams ....
raising money for ....
other ....

Out of school, ... has been commended by .... for ....
....

83

Table 3.23: continued

Your daughter's personal and social qualities

I have discussed with .... her attitudes towards studying, how she feels she gets on with

other people, and the pride she takes in her appearance. She thinks ....

....

....

....

Signed .... Form Tutor

Any other comments:

Signed ....

Chapter Four

STAFF DEVELOPMENT

A programme of staff development was perceived to be an essential feature in implementing records of achievement in our school. Staff development is usually seen as a continuous process whereby a school seeks to enable teachers to continue learning so that they can keep up with curriculum development and thus feel increasingly confident in their present work. It is also concerned with the preparation of teachers for the possible development of their careers. And whilst attempting to satisfy the professional and individual needs of teachers, staff development also exists to meet organisational needs so that the school can function effectively. A school where staff expect to be involved in professional development is one in which change is far more likely to be accepted and tried out with a certain amount of willingness.

By the end of the Spring term, we had reached a position where the working party, whilst trying to keep other teachers in the picture through feedback from meetings and from drawing up the skills and comment banks, had had far more opportunity than the rest of the staff to think through and talk about what was involved in profiling. It was a matter of some priority, since the innovation was to affect the majority of the teachers and all the First Year pupils, that the school's management team and the working party investigated ways of putting across to the staff as a whole the ideas on which they had been working. In particular, we needed:

(1) to increase staff awareness of the principles underlying records of achievement

(2) to facilitate the development of professional skills to cope with the emerging concepts

(3) to promote an understanding of the technicalities of how the system would be implemented

(4) to enable departmental procedures to be negotiated by the teachers concerned.

Since one of the most important functions of management is to reconcile the needs of the organisation with those of the individual, the management of the process of developing profiling within the school had to take account of introducing quite considerable organisational change while also giving teachers the skills necessary to deal with the concepts. Understanding how the system would work was every bit as important as trying to get to grips with understanding what it was all about, although of the two, the former was possibly easier to grasp than the latter. On the other hand, if a theoretical understanding was not reached, profiling would be approached as a mechanical exercise from which participants might derive little benefit.

HMI, in discussing 'Ten Good Schools', pointed out that 'what (these schools) have in common is effective leadership and a climate which is conducive to growth'. Additionally the report emphasised the importance of 'consultation, team work and participation'.

We have looked at organisational climate in the first chapter when the characteristics of schools were related to the sort of environment in which change, and professional growth can take place. Bearing this and the comments of HMI in mind, the management responsibilities in facilitating the smooth implementation of our innovation would include:-

(1) creating an open climate in which staff will feel free to say what they think about things

(2) setting up structures which encourage staff participation in making decisions that will affect them

(3) prioritising the needs of the organisation in consultation with colleagues

(4) providing active support in the form of time, resources, authority (if and when necessary)

(5) providing moral support and belief in what is being undertaken.

Relating these considerations to what had been done in

school, and remembering that open channels of communication already existed through the records of achievement working party, the next major responsibility of the management team was to consult with staff through the newly set up INSET committee to ascertain how they felt about using time in school to produce an INSET programme to cover both staff and institutional needs. The committee decided unanimously that records of achievement should be the first priority on our list for in-service education, and so it was agreed that the records of achievement working party should form a subcommittee of staff who were particularly interested in working on a programme of INSET for the whole staff. We felt that, for this occasion, we had sufficient resources amongst our own teachers to cope with undertaking the training and probably did not need to bring in outside speakers. At that meeting it was decided to set aside two afternoons for whole staff INSET and follow this up with separate departmental meetings. The afternoons would be in April and early May, just in time for the project to be a viable proposition for implementation in the summer term, and would run from 1.30 to 4.30pm, following a school day condensed into the morning.

The support and encouragement of the Head Teacher lent the necessary authority and moral support to the afternoons, and it was clear that everyone was expected to waive any other activities in favour of attending. In the event, only two or three teachers, out of a staff of nearly fifty, missed the afternoons and that was the unavoidable result of examination supervision or GCSE training.

Havelock et al. (1973), in a major study of the research literature on innovation, has discussed three main models: the Research, Development and Diffusion Model; the Social Interaction Model and the Problem Solving Model. Of these, the Problem Solving Model most closely parallels our introduction of profiling; it is fundamentally based on user need, which is 'translated by him (the user) into a problem statement and diagnosis ... the client is then able to conduct a meaningful search and retrieval of ideas and information which can be used in formulating or selecting the innovation' (Havelock, op.cit.).

This kind of innovation arises from the thinking and work of teachers in schools and from a need to respond to their observations; it is centred firmly in the individual school and so takes account of particular circumstances and characteristics; it is recognised as a 'bottom-up' model rather than a 'top-down' one. In so far as our introduction of profiling has come about from the need to develop an effective process throughout the pupil's school career in order to support the national move towards records of achievement for fifth years it is user oriented, and as such it seeks to solve the problems which it encounters in trying to bring about change. It has much in common with the following description taken from an American study of educational innovation:-

The problem-solving that characterises the initiation of change for the ideal adaptive school system has three main elements:

(a) The response to external pressures for change is proactive in the sense that it typically anticipates external demands and prepares a local solution before 'exogenous shocks' become local crises.

(b) Internal demand for change is continually stimulated and considered as legitimate. Needs are assessed and problems are identified on an on-going basis.

(c) ... staff of all levels participate in the proposal. By doing so, they can develop a sense of ownership in and commitment to the specific planned changes, and, more importantly in the long run, a sense of trust in the organisation's willingness to change'. (M.W. McLaughlin, 1976).

As R. Bolam (1982) pointed out, it is unlikely that any school would show all of these characteristics, but that some schools would be able to identify with some of them, for some of the time.

M. Eraut (1972) has pointed out that 'self-initiated and self-applied innovation will have the strongest user commitment and the best chances for long term survival'. We feel that the staff, through the working party, have been very involved in the process of introducing records of achievement, and that because it has been a teacher focused development, there will be commitment to it. The fact that teachers - and not managers or administrators or a remote body of planners - have worked at the project, should mean that it has been planned in the context of what is known about the school and that idiosyncratic factors have been taken into account. It can also be assumed that as far as possible in such a time-intensive exercise, the time factor will have been rendered as workable as possible, because all those who helped to put it together also have to use it, and so from a practical point of view they will want to ensure that it will work.

All this applies equally to the design of the INSET programme. R. Schmuck (1980), in referring to in-service programmes which have been systematically documented and evaluated, pointed out that 'training should involve much more than the presentation of knowledge through lectures and reading. Successful in-service programmes provide opportunities for participants to experience cognitive, attitudinal and behavioural change'. Thus the structure of such a programme must include opportunities for teachers to explore, in communication with others, their 'attitudes and feelings (about) the new information and its implication for changes in their role' (Schmuck, op.cit.).

M. Eraut (op.cit.) has referred to problem awareness and problem study as being an essential part of INSET, and has shown that a workshop approach to carrying out the in-service education is more conducive to attitudinal change than for instance the conference mode of delivery, which involves answers being given to passive receivers, rather than, as in a workshop, participants taking an active part in finding their own solutions to problems.

So when we came to plan our INSET, we had to decide first of all what our mode of delivery was to be. We felt we could work from where the staff 'were now', and we favoured a workshop approach so that teachers could participate actively in it. We felt that there would be commitment from the staff if everyone, regardless of status, worked together, and that the experience of learning was a whole lot different from being told how to do it. Since attitudes are only likely to change as a result of experiencing different ways of doing things, the experiential nature of the INSET was thought to be an important aspect of it.

A subcommittee of four teachers was formed to plan the two afternoons, and having had experience from other courses, we had several ideas which could be used. The first part of the planning, though, was to work out what we thought would be most useful for the staff to experience, and then to structure it systematically. Referring back to the work of R. Schmuck, we felt that we would like to offer the opportunity for teachers to think about, and consider their feelings towards what records of achievement are and what effects they might have generally in school, so we needed some activity which would encourage that to happen. We also thought it was an essential part of the exercise to structure the opportunity for contrary points of view to be voiced, for it is only by allowing such conflict to surface that it can be recognised and faced. If conflict is not recognised, it can seem like a denial of its existence, and can lead to an undercurrent of complaints, disagreement and dissatisfaction festering unhappily and threatening the whole enterprise. L. Stenhouse pointed out that 'change often comes through conflict within a staff; but it is important for the leadership of the school to recognise squarely what is happening and to manage conflict within the school rather than to pretend it does not exist' (op. cit.).

At this stage I discussed our ideas with the SERA project team, who are experienced in delivering INSET in pilot schools, so that they could help us to clarify our thoughts and to see whether they had used any materials which were consistent with our main concerns. They referred me to the work of Stephen Munby of the Sunderland TVEI team, who had drawn up a fairly complex activity which covered all we wanted to deal with, and which had been experienced by the SERA team at the conference of the National Association For Pastoral Care in Education (NAPCE) in November, 1986.

There are three strands to this INSET activity. The first involves working in groups to prioritise a list of statements about records of achievement - clarifying what is meant, what we feel about them, disagreeing or agreeing with them. During this time, one of the group has been working independently and observing group members as they work. The second part of the group activity is to assess each member along a checklist of skills which she or he might have displayed whilst working. The third strand of the INSET is that the observer/(teacher)/assessor is designated a different degree of negotiation with the group over his/her assessment of their skills on a scale of one to five. This works as follows: if the assessor was with group one, then s/he has no contact with the group other than to observe and assess them; s/he would not discuss his/her results with group members - in fact s/he has to withdraw from the group immediately after the assessments are given. At the other end of the scale if the assessor is with group five, s/he discusses the nature of the task with them from the outset, and as a group, including the assessor, they work out how they wish to proceed.

Our committee liked this idea as it incorporated the things which we wanted to do; it provided opportunity for clarifying ideas, for assessment of personal and social skills, and for negotiation - or a prescribed lack of it. However, when we looked carefully at it, we decided that the concept in its entirety was too complex for us to administer, and we were concerned that the points made by the degree of negotiation allowed which were of particular value, might escape unnoticed if the feedback happened to be insufficiently detailed and skilful. We thought the exercise would be of less value for the members of the non-participatory groups whose experience in negotiation procedures would have been negligible. Although the awareness of the need to negotiate/discuss assessments may have increased as a result of the activity, the thinking may have stopped there, and this would have been of concern for any of the teachers taking part, but particularly so if members of these groups included disaffected members of staff, as there may not have been the incentive to find out more.

So we decided to adopt the idea to suit our purposes better. We used two categories of assessor/observer only, rather than the original five, with our groups, structuring it so that one set of groups had the opportunity to engage in discussion with their assessor, while the other groups did not.

Having decided that this would be our main INSET activity, we next had to consider the organisation and administration of the afternoon. The planning needed to be very detailed as forty-five teachers were expected to attend and they would be expecting their afternoon to cover a lot of ground and to be smoothly executed. For our part, the fact that the group was so large posed the most intractable problem, both administratively in planning the different stages of the afternoon, and organisationally as there would be too many people to come together for a debriefing session based on whole group discussion. Ideally this is what we would have liked as it would have enabled us to hear and perceive people's comments and feelings about what they had been doing.

So the detailed planning began and was gone through with a fine tooth comb and refined many times before we were satisfied with the finished product. It became apparent that we would need 'leaders' at times during the afternoon,

91

and, although the members of the committee had not bargained for this onerous position at the start of our work, they accepted their inevitable role - though not without some misgivings! Teachers are well enough used to managing children in the classroom, but when it comes to managing teachers, particularly their own colleagues, this is a quite different challenge.

We found that not only did we have to plan the educational side of the afternoon, but also the domestic arrangements loomed quite large. There was the selection of rooms - which room was large enough to house the whole staff, but also near enough to a clutch of other rooms so that we should not have to disperse widely and lose cohesiveness? Once the rooms were selected, we realised that we would need overhead projectors and the urns for the tea to be carried over; and milk, tea and biscuits to be bought - and all this needed to be organised. We wanted to provide tea and biscuits because we felt they would be appreciated, but we did not want to schedule an off-site break (i.e. in the staff room) because of the loss of continuity to the programme, so the problem of actually making the tea presented an additional small problem to be sorted out. At lunchtime on the INSET day, having worked an extended morning, we would need to rearrange the rooms and take over papers, pens and card to be ready to start by 1.30 pm.

We started our educational planning by deciding on our aims for the afternoon which were outlined on the programme as follows:

- to give opportunity for staff to talk through their feelings about records of achievement
- to examine the significance of the issues involved
- to work together as a group
- to evaluate own contribution to the group
- to negotiate with colleagues on assessment of personal skills and qualities demonstrated
- to work with colleagues to help them assess their contribution to the group
- to experience feelings associated with different levels of participation in assessment.

Following a short introduction on the philosophy of records of achievement, we wanted to move straight into an activity which would help people to relax, to get them talking to different people, and to start them thinking along the lines of what we were about to do. Since we needed groups of five, our introductory activity was to organise these through a picture jigsaw of five pieces. Each person took one piece of a picture and had to find the holders of the other four pieces. Once found, the group was asked to split into a three and two, on the basis of similarities - for example, that two went together because they were wearing turquoise skirts and the others were not. They then linked up as a different five, and so the game went on for a short while. As it developed, people were encouraged to differentiate on the basis of characteristics which might not be so obvious as what they were wearing, such as people who laugh at the same things, or who share an interest in weight-lifting, or who can speak other languages, etc. Once the whole staff was thoroughly mixed up, they were asked to sit down in their final fives, to discuss what they thought the purposes of the activity had been and to feed back briefly to the whole group.

Once we were satisfied that the point of the exercise had been clarified, the groups were each asked to number its members from one to five. The only purpose in this was that, unknown to them at the time, the 'number threes' were to become the assessors, and we wanted the people selected for that position to be a perfectly arbitrary choice. By this time, we were ready to go into the main activity of the afternoon, so the assessors were withdrawn to be briefed in other rooms, and instructions for the rest of the staff were given as follows (see Table 4.1 for the list of statements):

Please read through the list of statements provided. When you have done this, your task is to:

(a) identify those statements with which you disagree and write their numbers in the appropriate box
(b) identify the ten statements with which you agree most strongly, and write their numbers in the other box.

You have ten/fifteen minutes for this exercise.

When the fifth person returns to your group, you should begin to negotiate within the group an agreed list of:

(a) the ten most important statements about recording achievement

(b)   those statements with which you all disagree

You should write these out in full on the sheet of card provided; they will be shared with the other groups later. You have 30 minutes for this exercise. N.B. During this group exercise, an observer will be assessing some of the skills and qualities that you display.

It was from the start of this activity onwards that the administration of the afternoon needed to be particularly sharp, and members of the INSET planning committee were metamorphosised into leaders who had to explain the tasks to the three separate groups of people. Assessors 'A' and assessors 'B' had moved into other rooms to be briefed on their roles, (see Tables 4.2 and 4.3), while the rest of the staff were urged to digest their own instructions. None of the group 'A's were allowed any discussion or negotiation with their assessors, while group 'B's not only had the opportunity to negotiate their assessments with the assessors, but also they were informed by their assessors exactly what was going to happen during the group activity. Once briefed, assessors collected their groups, took them to the allotted room and discussion began on the statements. Group 'B's were self-sufficient as the assessor had explained the procedures to them; they worked through prioritising the statements, moving on to the peer group assessment when they were ready, and taking tea while they continued working. The group 'A's completed the first part of the exercise, took a tea break, and then were instructed that the second part of the activity was to assess each other against a checklist of social and personal skills and qualities which had been demonstrated whilst they had been talking. The checklist can be seen in Table 4.4.

So the main activity of the afternoon was accomplished and had taken approximately an hour and a half. Quite as important as the activity, however, was the discussion on it which followed. The INSET planning committee was anxious that the staff should not just engage in talking about what records of achievement mean and experiencing peer group assessment, but that somehow the differences in the assessor's roles should be made apparent and discussion shoud arise as to the effects that these roles had on the groups. It was difficult to plan this because of the large numbers of staff involved, but we eventually decided that if each group A joined a group B the resultant group of ten people could undertake a discussion which would be structured to probe some of the foreseeable issues and no doubt others would arise as the discussion proceeded. To prepare the groups for this, each was given a time allowance of 20 minutes and asked to talk through and record their thoughts on an overhead transparency on the following questions:

(a) How did you feel when you knew you would be assessed?
(b) How did you feel about the way in which the assessment was done?
(c) Did group members become more self-aware?
(d) How did the assessors feel?

We hoped this would enable the discussion to range around the issue of how a person feels on being assessed; whether the participants had felt apprehensive or calm depending on the way the assessment was managed; whether they felt they wanted the opportunity to talk to their assessor and were not allowed to do so; whether they had become more aware of the ways in which they relate to other people in group work through the peer group profiling. And finally, did the assessors feel satisfied with their role, or would they have liked greater or lesser participation?

Armed with these thoughts, the groups then joined their partner group, (group A + group B), to discover what the others had been doing. The four groups which resulted from this manoeuvre were led in discussion by members of the INSET planning committee. The leader's duties in structuring the discussion, for which 20 minutes were allowed, were as follows:

(a) Ask each group to describe what they did.
(b) Make sure the differences between the two are well defined.
(c) Ask one group to talk through their feelings as detailed on the OHT.
(d) Ask the other group to do the same.
(e) Ask for comments/comparisons on their experiences.
(f) What do they think the exercise showed, in connection with assessing adults. Are there any differences when assessing children?

Finally all groups came together for a very brief summing up of the afternoon, and a request that everyone completed an evaluation form (Table 4.5), which, as we had over-run our time, people took home to do and some returned them and some did not.

EVALUATING THE INSET

It was clear, both from the afternoon, and through the next few days that the INSET had sparked off much discussion. Many of the worries about profiling were being voiced but also some of the advantages could be seen more clearly as a result of the experiential learning. The INSET showed that the staff were at many different stages of thinking about profiling, some of which were related to their overall pedagogic beliefs and values and some to their knowledge and understanding of the concepts involved.

The evaluation sheets and the considerable verbal feedback showed that the aims of the INSET had been achieved for most people, although some felt that the aims were so wide-ranging that one or two of them had not been fulfilled. For instance, some said that they had not had time for probing 'feelings' about records of achievement as they were so busy sorting out what the statements meant or implied, that they did not get further than that, although prioritising them may have opened up some feelings perhaps without the participants being really aware of what was happening.

The issues which caused the most discussion were

(1)   the personal skills assessment checklist
(2)   prioritising of the statements
(3)   the role of the assessor
(4)   how can it work in our school?

As these issues are directly related to introducing profiling into schools it is a useful exercise to look at the discussion opened up by this activity.

(1)   **the personal skills assessment checklist.** This seemed to be the most controversial aspect of the activity and showed that comments could be inappropriate to the assessment exercise, and that this is unsatisfactory, and to some extent annoying, for the participant. Having said this, inappropriate skills, such as 'is a creative person' and 'dependable', were

quite deliberately included in the personal skills profile so that this point would be brought out very clearly. On the other hand, it is sometimes not until a checklist is used that the inappropriateness becomes apparent, or can be fully understood. And it was interesting to see that some of the skills/qualities in the checklist were thought by some groups to be assessable and appropriate while these same skills/qualities were considered by other groups to be quite inappropriate. This raises the question of the level of awareness within a group; it could have been, for instance, that individuals were not noticing or reacting to non-spoken signals from others, but that does not necessarily mean that nonverbal communication was not taking place - just that it was not recognised as such or that it was being ignored or that there was a lack of agreement within the group of semantic understanding.

The discussion on the checklist, which will be further investigated in the next chapter, highlighted the fact that an essential prerequisite to drawing up lists of skills, or comment banks, is to be clear about the skills which are to be assessed in the first place.

(2) **prioritising the statements.** Sorting out the statements describing records of achievement into those with which the group agreed and those with which they disagreed involved establishing what was meant by the words in the first place, and then putting them into some sort of order. The most pressing request from the staff afterwards was - are there right and wrong statements, and if so, in what order of priority should they have been put?

Some of the statements were agreed on by most groups. These included that the statements should be written in simple language; that the profiling process should be part of a programme of social and personal development; that the criteria on which assessments are based should be clear to students and teachers from the start; and that the records of achievement should be for all students. The statements with which many people disagreed were that teachers have always negotiated with students when they discuss their work with them; and that employers and parents prefer plain examination results to records of achievement.

I think it is significant to look at what was left out of the staff priorities, as these omissions may give a clue as to the substance of further INSET which may be needed. Many of the other named priorities of the groups were important, but in comparison with the basic tenets, they could perhaps be considered to be peripheral, in the sense that, if the basics were present, then other things would automatically fall into place, and therefore, in a limited list, did not need to be itemised. For instance, to be consistent with the principles of recording achievement outlined earlier in this book, important considerations are that it should encourage pupils to reflect on the process of learning; that the learning process will be enhanced by a more democratic teacher/pupil relationship; that positive statements only should be used; and that pupils working in groups to assess themselves will alleviate (though not necessarily cure) the problem of where we can find the time to do this. So perhaps we may gather from this that the idea of right or wrong does not apply so much as whether the staff thinking is moving towards a clearer understanding of the central concepts.

3. **the role of the assessors.** It was interesting to watch the assessors in their roles and to compare what seemed to be happening in the different groups. Since we had all the group 'A's in one room and all group 'B's together in another room, it was easy to see the two different approaches. In the group A room, where the assessors did not communicate with their groups, we sensed a tenseness about the atmosphere that did not prevail in the other room. Also the need for a tea break in the group 'A' room was in sharp contrast to the fact that group 'B's managed to keep going without apparently wanting to have a break from what they were doing. The assessors of the 'A' groups actually retired from the room and were relieved to talk to and to gain reassurance from each other, whereas the assessors of the 'B' groups seemed to be well integrated with the other group members and did not appear to need a break.

The feedback from the overhead transparencies showed that there were standard worries about being assessed, although some groups which had been given the checklist to look at ('B' groups only) covered this by commenting that once they knew it consisted of positive qualities rather than negative ones, they stopped worrying about it. But both 'A' and 'B' groups voiced concern that the assessors might not be able to do their jobs fairly because of the extensive nature of the checklist and the number of people they had to assess. More of the 'A' groups indicated unease with their assessment procedures than did the 'B' groups, complaining of feeling nervous, apprehensive, worried, suspicious - especially at first - and particularly wary of assessing colleagues as they would have been reluctant to upset anyone in their group. A particularly important point which came across from both types of group but especially the 'A' groups, was the necessity of a full explanation of what they were expected to do, and what was going to happen, *before* the activity was started. Many of the 'A' groups felt they were going through the motions of an exercise without being informed what it was for, and this annoyed them! They would have felt more at ease if they had known what was going on, and one group actually stated: 'The whole *point* could have been explained better.' Yet, how often do we as teachers explain the purpose of an exercise to our classes?

The final point about the role of assessor was made by some 'A' groups who would have preferred to negotiate final assessments. Stress was laid both by the groups and by the assessors on trying to get the assessment 'right'. But 'rightness' must depend, amongst other things, on each person's perceptions of what actually happened and his/her own value system, thus supporting the view that negotiation might present a more balanced concept of 'rightness' to the participants.

4) **how can it work in our school?** A lot of thinking had started on how all this can be applied to our own situation, and in the written evaluations worries surfaced about the time factor, about negotiation, about assessment and about peer group assessment. These are complex issues of such importance that it is not possible in a few words to do justice to them; in fact they became the central feature of our second afternoon of INSET and this will be discussed in the next chapter.

CONCLUSIONS

The afternoon of INSET proved to be a valuable experience for most people in that it provided the opportunity to work together as a staff in addressing the complex issues involved in understanding records of achievement and developing the necessary skills to cope with it. The main conclusions we were able to draw from the afternoon are summarised as follows:

1. that the skills or qualities assessed should be appropriate to the exercise
2. that it is more satisfying for the assessed person to know in advance the skills/qualities on which she is being assessed.
3. that it is more satisfying and less threatening to be able to discuss assessments than not to be allowed to do so.
4. that it is less threatening if the skills assessed are positive.

In the next chapter, we shall look in more detail at some of the other assessment issues which arose from the thinking of one or two of the groups as well as developing the general theme of negotiation and what we actually understand by it.

Table 4.1: Personal Recording - The Issues

(1) a personal record should record only unambiguous statements
(2) should not give much extra work to teachers
(3) should be for all students, whatever their academic ability
(4) should be geared to have a catalytic effect on the curriculum
(5) should include only positive statements about students
(6) should be written in language the students can understand
(7) should include statements about personal qualities
(8) should include out of school experiences
(9) should include examination results
(10) should only record information which is agreed between student and teacher
(11) should include negative statements if those statements are true
(12) should allow for peer group assessment and negotiation
(13) should be part of an overall programme of personal and social development
(14) should include assessment of cross-curricular skills
(15) should be written statements and not ticks in boxes
(16) should not be done at fixed intervals
(17) students who assess their experiences and achievements will be more motivated in their courses of study
(18) personal recording does not have to be a purely individual exercise
(19) the personal record belongs to the student
(20) employers and parents prefer plain examination results to records of achievement
(21) teachers have always 'negotiated' with students when they discuss work with them
(22) personal records will have little validity because the students have drawn them up
(23) students working in groups to assess themselves will help to alleviate the time problem
(24) the personal record is essentially for students to reflect on the process of learning
(25) the criteria for assessment must be clear to students and teachers from the start
(26) the learning process will be facilitated and enhanced by a democratic teacher/student partnership
(27) students who review and reflect on their own

Table 4.1: continued

experiences and achievements will be more successful in life outside and beyond school.

Disagree with:

Agree with:

These materials have been adapted from an original package by Stephen Munby and the Sunderland TVEI team, and from an exercise undertaken at a National Association for Pastoral Care Conference on Records of Achievement held in 1985.

Table 4.2: Recording Achievement Workshop Group A

Observer/assessor's brief

Your task is as follows:

1) Observe your group as they are discussing and negotiating their priorities for recording achievement.
2) Use the checklist provided to identify the skills and qualities demonstrated by individuals in your group during this exercise.
3) YOU MUST NOT COMMUNICATE WITH YOUR GROUP AT ANY TIME DURING THIS EXERCISE.
4) You must decide for yourself what criteria you will use when you attribute particular skills or qualities to individuals within your group.
5) You must only identify and record skills and qualities which are demonstrated during the group priorities for recording achievement exercise.
6) At the end of the exercise, the group members will be asked to assess each other's performance, using identical checklists to yours. You may observe this discussion, and you may wish to alter your own assessments in the light of what is said by the group, but you must not communicate with your group during this activity.
7) Once the group has completed the peer group profiling activity - or by 3.20 pm - you must read out to the group your assessment of their performance, using your checklist as a guide. You may explain your assessment if you wish to but no negotiation or discussion is allowed with your group.
8) After you have read out your assessment, you should withdraw to G1.

These materials have been adapted from an original package by Stephen Munby and Sunderland TVEI.

Table 4.3: Recording Achievement Workshop Group B

Observer/assessor's brief

Your task is as follows:

1)   Explain to your group that you have been asked to observe the group, and to identify the skills and qualities demonstrated by them during their discussions about the priorities for recording achievement.
2)   Give each member of the group a copy of the checklist and ask them to read it.
3)   Explain to the group that after they have negotiated the priorities for recording achievement they will all have an opportunity to do some peer group profiling.
4)   Explain to the group that during the peer group profiling exercise you will become a member of the group with no more authority than any other group member. No skills or qualities will be accredited to any individual unless every member of the group agrees.
5)   Once the group have understood all this, they can begin the negotiation of their priorities for recording achievement. During this activity you must use the checklist to identify the skills and qualities demonstrated by the individuals in your group.
6)   You must decide for yourself what criteria you will use to judge whether a group member has demonstrated a particular skill or quality.
7)   The group should have identified their priorities for recording achievement by approximately 2.50. You can break for tea if you wish from 2.50 - 3.00 pm, and the peer group profiling exercise should be completed by 3.25 pm.

These materials have been adapted from an original package by Stephen Munby and Sunderland TVEI.

Table 4.4: Assessment Checklist

Group Members 1 2 3 4 5					Assessment Checklist
					notices and reacts to non spoken signals from others
					reacts thoughtfully and sensibly to criticism from others
					discusses with others in order to reach agreement
					listens attentively to what others are saying
					questions others for clarification of their ideas
					is a creative person
					thinks of new ideas
					is willing to consider other ideas and opinions
					can fit into a new situation
					can use existing skills in new situation
					prepared to change her mind as a result of discussion
					is ready to start straight away
					is willing to be the leader
					summarises what has been said from time to time
					works easily with others
					keeps to the point
					has a lively sense of humour
					makes only positive comments
					dependable
					is prepared to ask for explanation if she doesn't follow

Table 4.5: Evaluation

1. Do you feel that this course was successful in fulfilling its aims?
2. If yes, which parts of the course were significantly useful for you?
3. If no, which of the aims were not fulfilled for you?
4. If no, which part of the course was the least productive for you?
5. Which of the methods used were
(a) helpful for your learning?
(b) unhelpful for your learning?
(c) why?
6. Can you think of ways in which you could apply some of this learning to how you will manage next term's recording process for first year pupils?
7. Do you have any specific requests that you would like covered in the next INSET session on Records of Achievement?

Chapter Five

ASSESSMENT AND NEGOTIATION

The experiential nature of the INSET was valuable in helping
staff to perceive some of the issues concerning recording
achievement more clearly. Assessment was one of these
issues, and through the experience of using a self-
assessment checklist, teachers benefited from seeing some
of the key points of which to be aware in drawing up such
lists, but negotiation was seen as another issue, and loomed
as a huge problem from at least two points of view. First,
negotiation was seen to be a very time-consuming activity,
and second, teachers doubted that they had the requisite
skills to accomplish it effectively. One of the formidable
questions which came across in the evaluation was how were
we going to be able to take time out of our already tight
schedules of work to talk individually to children about their
skills and achievements, particularly when we had classes of
31 to deal with? Following closely on this came the question
that if the child did not agree with our assessment of her
attitudes or skills and we were unable either to change our
position or shift hers as a result of discussion, what were we
to do? Should we change the assessment to be in keeping
with our professional opinion or should we agree to differ
and leave the assessment off the profile altogether?

These and other questions will be addressed in this
chapter, but I should like to start by going back to
assessment, and before proceeding further, to look at what
we understand by the term 'assessment'. We assess each
other frequently in our daily encounters with people, in that
we observe how they behave towards us and others; we hear
what they say, we see what they do and consequently we
guess at what their values, beliefs and attitudes seem to be;

we respond to them as a result of interpreting our observations of their verbal and non-verbal communications. Rowntree (1977) has said of assessment in education, that it

> ... can be thought of as occurring whenever one person, in some kind of interaction, direct or indirect, with another, is conscious of obtaining and interpreting information about the knowledge and understanding, or abilities and attitudes of that other person. To some extent or other it is an attempt to <u>know</u> that person.

Self-assessment, then, can be seen as the process by which a person becomes more aware of her abilities and attitudes, and so comes to know and understand herself better.

If we return to the experience of self assessment which formed part of the activity during our afternoon of INSET, the points which were raised and discussed in depth in groups and which are vital to a real understanding of profiling personal skills and qualities included the following:

- some comments on the list were ambiguous
- some were inappropriate
- comments were positive only
- there may have been too many comments
- assessment was limited to specific skills and qualities only
- there is a need to know the criteria on which assessment is based
- inappropriate criteria may lead to inappropriate activity
- positive assessment for only one member implies negative assessment for others
- <u>a series of assessments is essential because a participant who did not show a particular skill might show it on another day or in a different situation.</u>

To enable an assessment checklist of skills and qualities to be used effectively, much effort should be made to ensure that descriptive statements are unambiguous. Statements are better composed as a group activity as an individual does not always see ambiguity in phrases which s/he chooses, whereas subjecting the statements to the probing of several minds often eliminates those whose meanings are not clear. Being *dependable* is an example of ambiguity on our personal skills profile. People recognise differing degrees of dependability, and different interpretations of what it actually means anyway. It could mean 'always there', as in not having to leave the room for anything; it could mean 'always ready to say something to help conversation along'; it could mean 'is a reassuring person to have around' which begs the question in what ways is s/he reassuring to have around?; it could mean 'can be relied upon not to argue' but then, how valuable is this in terms of personal and group development?

Dependable is liable to too many differing interpretations and as such, it does not seem to be performing any useful function. The concept of dependability itself needs clarification before a decision is made to include it, and if it is then thought to make a worthwhile contribution to the profile, the words describing it should be chosen with care. Plainly, *dependable* is not adequate as it stands.

Another ambiguous statement is *can use existing skills in new situation* - ambiguous because we are not in a position to know what existing skills the assessor has in mind. It could be assumed that the person being assessed was using existing skills, but are they the same skills that another person is showing, and if they are, is this relevant or not? Unless the existing skills are identified such a statement does not make much sense to the assessor; even if they are identified, the assessor does not know whether the participant has achieved these skills before, or whether s/he is just trying them for the first time. There would seem to be a need here to be far more specific to enhance understanding for both the assessor and the participant.

Statements about skills or qualities can also suffer from being inappropriate, as in *is a creative person*. In this exercise, only the skills and qualities which were demonstrated should have been recorded, and it is not reasonable to assume that someone is a creative person on the basis of observing her/him for one half hour session. In any event, 'being creative' has something in common with 'being dependable' which we looked at previously. What do we understand by a 'creative person'? Is being creative to do with having ideas, and if so, how many ideas make her a creative person? Do all assessors have an identical understanding of the criteria which determine a 'creative person', and if they do not, which seems likely to be the case, will this not allow for considerable variation in whether a participant gains this attribute, with the possibility of unfortunate repercussions on some sensitive self-concepts of those who do not? For if we say that someone is a creative person on the basis of what the assessor has seen of her/him, but others in the group are not given this accolade, it might be inferred that they are not creative people, yet in different circumstances, they may paint wonderful pictures, or write poetry, or express themselves in dance. Much more appropriate, in place of *is a creative person* is *thinks of new ideas* because this describes what can be seen to be happening while the activity proceeds and does not generalise from one skill to a comprehensive assumption of a personal characteristic.

It could also be argued that *has a lively sense of humour* is inappropriate in the same sense, in that the statement does not describe what the participants did but rather what they are like. Perhaps *makes amusing comments* could take its place, but this could imply that the participant did not take the exercise seriously, whereas it was not the intention of the original comment *has a lively sense of humour* to be pejorative. So a decision has to be made on whether this statement is necessary to complete the picture of our assessment, and if we decide it is, then we will have to search around for a different way of saying it, remembering once we have done so, that although our statement is clearly unambiguous to us, it is always open to different interpretations by other people, who will bring to it their own set of values, attitudes, opinions, etc.

As we have seen, comments can fall into the trap of being not only inappropriate and/or ambiguous, but also generalisations from observations of specific behaviour. Profiles of personal and social skills and qualities are particularly prone to this condition, and when drawing up our First Year profile, we tried to avoid this happening. For instance when describing punctuality, to say that someone *is always punctual* based on the fact that she was not late for school during the year is not necessarily accurate. It could be that she was always punctual because her parent delivered her to school on time, but if left to her own devices, she may not be such an accurate timekeeper, or she may be punctual for some things, but not for others. There is less value judgement implied in describing the facts of the situation and leaving the reader - the pupil herself, parent, teacher, and later on, employer - to draw her/his own conclusions.

The skills or personal qualities on our checklist were

couched in positive terms only. Describing what a person does in positive terms is seen as a motivating factor and is perceived by the participants to be non-threatening, as was shown in the evaluation comments of our teachers. But the counter-argument is that it might be better to show participants what they are doing wrong, as well as what they are doing right, so that they can adapt their behaviour accordingly. If we look back to the unease expressed by our staff over the possibility of being assessed adversely, of not having the right of reply, of not wishing to hurt, upset or annoy their own colleagues during assessment, of needing to be able to trust the integrity of the assessor, of feeling they had to act with circumspection, then perhaps we should take these feelings into account when deciding whether to add negative statements to our list. To have added *talks too much* or *dominates the group* or *seems to listen only to own point of view* or *will not change her/his mind despite discussion* would have added considerably to the insecurity of the participants, and might have prejudiced pre-existing relationships. Negative statements would have led to disharmony amongst participants, with all the implications that entails both for present feelings and for working together in the future. If this applies to adults, it applies at least equally to children, who are endowed with the same sensitivities but with less experience of life to cope with their feelings, and so the situation has the potential for being even more unsatisfactory.

The use of positive rather than negative statements is consistent with Douglas McGregor's Y theory (1960) which posits the case that it is natural for people to want to work, and that 'commitment to objectives is a function of the rewards associated with achievement'. The theory lays stress on the positive aspects of the strivings of human beings rather than on the negative side of things, and belief in the philosophy being advanced here tends to predetermine that a manager's approach to people will see the good in them first, rather than be looking for their faults. Theory X, which suggests that most people dislike work and have to be cajoled into it through fear of punishment, that there is no intrinsic commitment to the organisation's objectives and that they prefer to be told what to do than to take that responsibility for themselves, is more in line with the use of negative statements to describe people's behaviour, where it is assumed that many participants will be difficult, concerned only with furthering their own views and therefore needing coercive direction towards adapting their skills and characteristics more favourably.

Theory Y also ties in with A. Maslow's hierarchy of human needs (1954) which points to the fact that people have needs which they seek to fulfil and at the highest level, this is seen in 'self-actualisation'. Social and ego needs which have a bearing on the theoretical aspects of profiling, include the need to belong to the group, to be accepted, to give and receive friendship, to develop self-esteem, and to sense recognition of the self in the way other people behave towards you. It is important for personal growth that these needs should be satisfied, which they will be more readily through a positive approach than a negative one.

Some of our teachers experienced this in action as they worked together in groups. Assuming that the skills and qualities being assessed would be those which enhance personal interactions and group work, they tried hard to participate and cooperate as a group, and in doing so, they were fulfilling social and ego needs to be accepted by fellow members of their groups, to develop self-esteem, and to fulfil the group's task effectively, thereby achieving recognition for success in their activities. One group declared that if they'd known at this stage the contents of the checklist, they would have attempted to create a situation to allow them to show their skills, even on inappropriate statements such as dependability - they thought they would have created an artificial situation so that they could show this quality. This is perhaps taking the idea to extremes whereas in reality it would not have happened, but the fact that it was even mentioned suggests that people may be enticed to work towards checklist skills and qualities however inappropriate they may be. Thus there is an onus on the part of those who draw up profiles to be aware that they may be encouraging prescriptive behaviour amongst the participants, and profiles need to be structured so that mistaken listing of inappropriate skills does not lead to their use during an activity.

A positive outcome of this is also worth considering, namely that groups can work towards the skills in such a way that desirable behaviour patterns might be circumscribed by judicious planning. For instance in group work we might like to select out the tendency to dominate or to bully. Carefully designed profiles and discussion, supported by consistency in the ethos and curriculum of the school, could contribute to leading children towards a finer understanding of sharing, of consideration for others and of cooperation; they could lead towards the need to achieve group approval for the individual, and as a consequence, the group would act in some measure as a regulator of individual behaviour.

All this points to the fact that although the skills and qualities are written in positive terms, there is a negative side to profiling. We have discussed the motivating force underlying positive statements - of fulfilling oneself and being accepted by one's peers - but the converse has not been spelled out. If a participant is recorded on a profile as having achieved a skill or having shown a particular personal quality, then that tells everyone something positive about that person during the activity. If however, the participant does not achieve one of the skills or qualities, this contributes a negative valuation at that time and in that situation. But instead of the profile saying perjoratively *keeps interrupting*, there would simply be an omission against *listens attentively to what others are saying*. The emphasis is different and allows the participant to retain self-respect whilst at the same time, discussion on the profile should offer the opportunity to look at why *listens attentively to what others are saying* failed to get a positive rating.

However, it is not sufficient simply to be aware of unsatisfactory behaviour patterns; they have to be faced, talked over, and strategies made to help to modify them. This is the target setting which is so crucial to the profiling process - merely amassing a lot of facts about skills and qualities is not necessarily going to help anyone's personal growth - it is the thinking about, planning of, decision making on and commitment to future aims which, if realistic, can support individual development.

Finally in this section on drawing up profiles, we should look at the problem of the quantity of skills and qualities to be listed. In our self-assessment activity on the INSET afternoon, some teachers complained that there were far too many skills to be assessed for the exercise to be accomplished properly. On the other hand, other members of staff claimed that, once an initial understanding was reached, the task of the assessor did not make excessive demands on her/him. So we would need to consider whether we could have managed with fewer skills to assess; and if we had managed with fewer, whether the picture of each person's performance would have been lacking in essential detail. This brings us to whether, by mistakenly overlooking them, we might have left out any important skills which really should have been included and also, how we could structure the assessment so that not just one, but a series of assessments over a period of time could be completed, in order to allow further opportunities for showing and developing skills.

As we pick up the issue of the possibility of restricting profiles in the interests of manageability, we are becoming more keenly aware of the different facets of assessment. We can see that we might be responsible for circumscribing what happens in an activity if value is attached only to what is seen to be assessed. And it works the other way also - that, as teachers, we may be so blinkered by our prescribed checklist that we may not observe valuable learning which lies outside our preconceived ideas of what should happen. This applies not only to the personal and social skills but also to the subject-specific and cross-curricular skills as well. So 'what to assess' and then 'how to assess it' begin to assume a theoretical significance which teachers may not have experienced in detail before.

OBJECTIVES, TESTING AND PROFILES

D. Rowntree (op. cit.) pointed to three types of learning objectives which are capable of being assessed, as cognitive - to do with thinking and the mind; affective - concerned with attitudes and feelings; and psychomotor - to do with muscular activity. Within these three objectives he further discussed levels of complexity, referring to Bloom's cognitive taxonomy (1956), and then moved on to present a 'coarse-grained schema' which he finds

quite useful in thinking about levels in relation to any particular content area:

1. Recalling facts or principles (eg What is an x?)
2. Applying a given or recalled fact or principle (eg How does x help you solve this problem?)
3. Selecting and applying facts and principles (from all that are known) to solve a given problem (eg What do you know that will help you solve this problem?)
4. Formulating and solving own problems by selecting,

generating and applying facts and principles (eg What do I see as the problem here and how can I reach a satisfying solution?)

At level 3 the student is choosing the means to a given end. At level 4, he is exercising at least some choice also about the end. Level 4 represents the student making his own meanings within his structure of ideas rather than performing tricks with other people's meanings ...

It is in looking at such a differentiation of levels of learning objectives that we may sharpen our thinking about what we are teaching, and about how to assess the pupils' learning. Thus there is scope for curriculum development as we refine our thinking on objectives and project it into our schemes of work and into the profiling process. A further problem exists, however, in ensuring that our assessment procedures actually test what we think they are testing. For instance, in mathematics, we may think we are testing for recall of a method learnt last week, but, unless we interpret the resultant work carefully, it could be that our testing is for accuracy as well as recall, because a pupil can get the answer wrong through inaccuracy, even though she remembered and used the method correctly. Similarly, whether a child can apply a principle to solving a problem will depend on whether she can recall the principle, unless that forms part of the given information. So in a situation which seeks to test the application rather than the recall, these need to be separated out and maybe a reminder to the child of the principle would enable an effective test to be made on its application.

If profiles are to be specific in recording the detail of assessments made of the learning objectives undertaken during the year, then there are other problems to be overcome, the most uncompromising of which is the time factor. But, leaving that aside for the time being, it is very important to realise that a profile based on detailed assessments demands that the means of assessment should faithfully reflect what it is seeking to test, as was shown in the mathematics examples described above. Having ensured as far as possible that this has happened, there will be a need to reduce the information received from the profile for a summative document and to collate it in manageable form for pupils, parents and teachers to read and digest. So the question arises as to what should be left out, which raises the thorny issue of which are the most worthwhile assessments, or whether what is recorded should be conflated to reduce the detail. The trouble with conflation is that the end product is frequently meaningless in the sense that disparate achievements are brought together and averaged out, telling the recipient nothing specific about the pupil through so doing. This lack of specificity has been one of the ongoing complaints about interpreting examination results, in that a mark of 50% does not make clear whether the pupil knew only half of what she 'should' have known, or whether she could answer only half of the questions on the examination paper and not the other half, or whether she only knew enough to give half an answer to each of the questions, or whether she expressed herself insufficiently clearly, or even whether she knew a lot more that didn't happen to fall under the scrutiny of the examiner. D. Rowntree (op. cit.) has pointed to the differentiation of students through the profiling process, and likened profiling to

> dividing the students out from one another like the opening out of a fan ... with a view to showing that each is in a class of his own - 'sui generis and unique'. Thereby, the recipient of the report is being put into a new and more human relationship with the assessors and the assessed. He is no longer encouraged to view the assessors as expert technocrats who will answer the question 'What's this student worth to everybody?' Rather he is being given a relativistic 'It all depends' - answer, one that throws him back on his own criteria which he can compare with those the assessors have applied, noticing that the student is, for him, good, bad or interesting in parts.

In drawing up formative profiles, the problems of designing effective assessment procedures, interpreting the results and recording them, all have to be addressed idiosyncratically by the school, and much will depend for the response on the resources available - including time, and the willingness and ability of the staff to think clearly through their teaching objectives, and to consider the consequent areas of what to assess, how to assess it and how to deal with the data so generated. It is clear from our experiences that there may be many different teacher-responses to these problems, so much informed discussion and investigation of possible alternatives should take place before hurtling into an early foreclosure on possible courses of action.

EXPERIENCES OF ASSESSMENT

Ideas on how best to assess pupils formed part of our second INSET programme, in which members of staff from different departments shared some of their experiences with us. We were particularly interested in the developing areas of self-assessment and peer group assessment, as, having experienced these in the previous INSET programme, staff were keen to know whether this sort of approach would be effective with our pupils. Several of the staff were sceptical that such assessment would work, not least because they felt children would not know how to set about assessing themselves, that they might over-rate themselves, or that they might comment adversely and unfairly on other pupils' work. However, staff who have undertaken peer group assessment were prepared to talk to us about what they had done, and two such case studies are described below.

Case Study One

We had worked during the year to encourage constructive criticism of any work presented or read to the class. This has taken a great deal of effort and reiteration of what we are looking for, but now, my first and second year classes do this fairly automatically and usually very thoughtfully.

I wanted to formalise this process and to develop the pupils' powers of self-assessment and ability to assess others. To this end, after some work which entailed presenting a short scene to the class, I gave the groups some points to help them in their first attempt to assess their achievement as a group. They were as follows:

1. Was there anything your group found hard to prepare? (ideas, people, etc.)
2. Did you all help each other to prepare the scene? Can you give an example of what someone did to help?
3. Do you think your group did the presentation well? Tell each other how well you think each person did.

4. Try to say which people did any of these things and say how well they did them:

   - listened carefully to everybody
   - gave helpful ideas
   - got people going if they were stuck
   - suggested more effective ways of doing something.

5. Finally, do you think that talking like this will help you to improve?

It should be noted that the stress in the assessment was on the preparation and not on the end product, and also that groups were keen to tape their discussions which they undertook to do by themselves. The first years began very hesitantly and did not really support each other early on, but were happy to talk about their cooperation. They used points which were suggested in the guidance notes, which reinforces the view that they need clear criteria with which to work.

I was interested to hear that they were at ease in admitting their difficulties or in criticising their own contributions. Gradually they relaxed, and began to organise their discussion. One suggested, pleasantly, to the quietest member so far, that she might like to begin the third question.

As they became more used to talking with each other in the presence of the tape, they began to range over the work of other groups in the class, and as part of this, comparing their own group with others. After a while one of the group felt that this was going away from the point and brought the discussion back to what she thought was relevant. At one point in time, one of the group becomes lost for words; the rest of the group wait, then rescue her, enabling her to respond.

I feel their comments on whether a teacher rather than peers should assess performance are interesting and certainly provide food for thought

Pupil A   It helps if a teacher doesn't tell you what you're doing wrong - but your friends tell you. If a teacher does it and says all these great big words, you don't really know what they mean and you think they're being rude or something ...

One other point which came out was that when there was disagreement about who should assess, opinions were expressed politely and fluently, which showed the critical development that had taken place during the last ten or so minutes of the discussion.

Pupil B   I think it is better when a teacher tells you what to do and criticises you in all your work because then you'll take it more seriously.

Pupil A   I don't think so, because if your friend says it, ... um ...

Pupil C   You can talk with her ...

Pupil A   Yes, and argue with her - but if a teacher says it you can't start shouting back at her or you'll get a detention or something

Pupil C   Sometimes if it comes from a teacher you don't take it to heart - you think - oh, that teacher doesn't like me.

Pupil A   Yes ...

Finally, there is a summing up of the points of view expressed.

Case Study Two

This assignment was given to Third Year pupils. It consisted of each person giving a talk which explained a process or an experience. An important element of the work was to be the extended comments of the 'audience' - the group. The group agreed their own assessment criteria as follows: content, nature of explanation, beginning and ending, general communication.

After the talks had been assessed by the group, each person was asked for a written evaluation of her experiences. It is interesting to see the following comments made in these evaluations as they supported the oral observations made after the lesson to the effect that the pupils had learned much from what their friends had said, and that they would like to do the same again!

The comments I got made me feel really good.
Everyone isn't as mean as I thought they would be.
Listening to the comments, if we were to give our talk again, we can learn from our mistakes.

I wished we hadn't gone first, because all the others learned from the comments and we couldn't.
Because of the comments I will know to improve my content.
I did not realise I had done so well.
It's good that the class says what they feel and that they don't criticise someone just because they don't like them.

It is clear from the things pupils have said in these two case studies, that for peer group assessment to be successful, the atmosphere in the classroom has to be conducive for the development of trust, both amongst pupils and also between teacher and pupils, as they will not speak openly if they suspect others will make fun of them or if they think that they will be shown to be 'in the wrong'. And it is the teacher who is responsible for creating that atmosphere of acceptance, support and constructive, helpful criticism without which peer group assessment is a non-starter.

DEPARTMENTAL POLICY ON ASSESSMENT

Many departments are looking at assessment in terms of how it can be most effectively organised and carried out, given that with the coming of profiles the process of assessment has become an integral part of the curriculum, instead of being an unqualified mark out of ten or a test tacked on at the end of term to see that learning has taken place. Profiles have opened the door to self-assessment and peer group assessment in the expectation that pupils will become more involved in their learning as they grapple with whether they feel they have achieved the assessment criteria and how they feel about the progress they are making. As we have seen above in the case studies, pupil involvement does seem to be heightened through giving them a say in assessing performance.

The English department, in its perception of recording achievement as being a process rather than an end product, has found itself involved in two fundamental reappraisals of policy, namely that the role of teacher/assessor has had to be reviewed, and that if children are to be expected to take part in the assessment process then they have to be taught how to assess work as this is not something they are automatically able to do. The review of the teacher role in assessment means that no longer will the teacher expect to give a mark, with or without a comment, to which a pupil would not be expected to respond. And, whereas in the past no-one except the teacher knew the criteria on which the mark was based, and in any event, the grade may have been a purely impressionistic one with no clear criteria, in future, the children will become used to knowing the skills that are being assessed, and the criteria are on which the assessment is based.

In helping the pupils to become involved in the process of self-assessment, the department has introduced a policy of commenting thoroughly on written work, which is not given a mark. The intention is that the child will read the comment carefully to find out what the teacher thinks of her work. Children are encouraged to own their work in the sense that they should feel free to challenge the teacher's comments and there is a rule that direct questions, either from the teacher or the child, must be answered. Encouraging such a dialogue means that the child begins to see that the teacher's comment is not always the final statement on her work and that it is all right to express her own point of view. By not giving a grade, the competitive element between children in class is lessened, thereby allowing a more supportive atmosphere to develop. The extended comments have been welcomed by parents as being useful in guiding them towards helping their children at home.

When setting a piece of work, it is important for the teacher to spell out exactly what is being looked for in the way of skills that have been used, and the criteria which will be used for the assessment. First Year pupils tend to feel safer if they can concentrate on one aspect only, for instance, in a creative essay the skill assessed might be character presentation or descriptive writing whereas in a letter, the skill being assessed might be accuracy in presentation, spelling, punctuation and grammar. Not only does the teacher assess the work, but pupils also are used to looking at their own work and responding to specific questions concerned with attitude, achievement, or effort, or they could be asked to evaluate their work in the form of an open-ended statement about how they feel about what they have done. At first, comments seem to be rather superficial, and they write what they think the teacher would like to see, but as they become more used to the activity, their comments have an air of a deeper truth about them. A checklist to be used by each pupil has been compiled, so that although only one skill might be assessed at any one time, the range of skills capable of application can be appreciated.

The experiences of this year have shown that First Year pupils are able to assess each other (as in case study one above), providing they are given clear guidelines as to the assessment criteria and how to compare their work to those criteria. They need to be taught that if they comment on other people's work, they must be able to substantiate their point of view with clear evidence, and that, even so, the evidence they cite could be interpreted quite acceptably, but differently, by other people. Teachers setting up peer group assessment in lessons would expect to intercede with questions designed to lead the group towards a clear understanding of the criteria, and of how closely the participants measure up to them; they would also give the participants the opportunity to follow up the comments made by other class members.

To sum up, the following features have been seen to be essential to the development of pupil self-assessment and peer group assessment:

1. teachers and pupils need to be clear about the skills and criteria for assessment - what is being looked for?
2. teachers (or pupils, as they become more skilful) should decide on an appropriate means of assessment; for instance, through an essay, a discussion, a presentation, a piece of drama, etc.
3. teachers need to issue guidelines about how to assess quality of work - how do we apply the criteria to the pupil's work?
4. there should be an environment in which work is discussed, judgements supported by evidence and assessments queried
5. the atmosphere should be supportive and non-competitive
6. the classroom should be one in which everyone feels she can express her opinion and the teacher will not automatically over-rule her
7. if the teacher feels an assessment is not fair, s/he will question, guide and negotiate until a more equitable perspective has been reached.

As part of the work the department has done on assessment, a Third Year group was set a piece of work which involved thinking about the reports which teachers have traditionally given to pupils, whether this procedure was satisfactory and if it could be improved. The discussion eventually centred around whether pupils were sufficiently informed, fair and objective to write their own reports, and the comments made by them reinforced many of the arguments which their teachers have been engaged in thinking about recently. It is interesting to see the pupils' perspectives from the following extracts, and to realise that the points of view which they are presenting, both for and against, are very close to the perspectives of many of their teachers.

What are the advantages of writing your own report?

You know what is being written about you.
You can say what you think.
You can question/discuss/adjust.
You can look at things a teacher is not always aware of.
Teachers and pupils can become more aware of how each other feels.
You become more involved in what you are doing because you had a say in what you did.

What are the disadvantages of writing your own report?

Some people will find it hard to write their own reports and to assess themselves because they will not know what to look for.
Pupils can under/overestimate themselves.
There will be arguments.
It will be hard to assess what everyone did in a group.
You would be lazy because you know you can write your own report.
You would be too modest.
You might not tell the truth - you could lie or exaggerate.
You wouldn't be as honest as your teacher would be.

How would writing your own report affect your work?

> It would make you think about your work - you 'confess' to yourself.
> You see you have to improve or you won't get any qualifications.
> Some people will not do anything.
> When you have more responsibility, you do better work.
> We wouldn't try so hard.
> We'll work harder, we will be proud we've got a good report by working hard all year.

Who is the best judge of your work?

> The best judge of your work is you, as you know your own capabilities.
> A combination of teacher and pupil.
> Teacher and pupil can put your ideas together and come up with a fair report.

Do you think it will change your relationship with your teacher?

> Pupils will become more independent and it will improve.
> The teacher would become more aware of your problems.
> The teacher's work would be easier. (!)
> We don't think it would change, they would still be telling you what to do.

What should the report have in it?

> Standard of work.
> Attitude.
> How you work - how you fit in.
> Behaviour.
> Exam. results.
> How you're getting on.
> Stuff for employers.

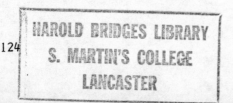

124

Who is the report for?

Us - so we can improve.
Us - parents, teachers and the people who give us jobs.

Comments which came up in discussion

When you leave school, people won't come up to you and tell you to sort yourself out; you've got to be able to do that for yourself.
We'll be honest, because we'll feel guilty if we're not.
The group will have to stop each other mucking about otherwise we'll all get bad marks.
Who will we be cheating if we lie? Just ourselves.

THE TIME FACTOR AND PROFILING

A profile consists of a range of assessments of the general skills, and personal and social qualities of the pupil, based on evidence which has been gathered, looked at, sifted and evaluated in pursuit of getting to know the pupil better and to record what is discovered about her. It is an attempt to describe where the pupil 'is now' and is a tool of reflection, helping her to develop insight into what she has achieved, and to make plans for the future, thereby contributing to personal growth. Thinking, however, takes time, and as time is not an infinite commodity, schemes of work need to be structured to take account of the process of reflection.

Teachers have always marked their pupils' work to provide feedback to them, to encourage them to work harder and to provide information for parents, teachers, colleges of further education and employers. They have used different methods - essays, examinations, tests, projects, exercises and so on, according to what they want to mark, be it descriptions, recall of information, creative writing, personal research, solving problems or whatever. But the mark has often been a letter grade or numerical mark out of ten/twenty with maybe a brief comment to substantiate or explain the teacher's thoughts and evaluation of the pupil's work. With the development of profiling have come changes in the way teachers 'mark' work, for, as we have seen, 'marking' has the potential to become a much more comprehensive system of assessing and reporting on pupils' work. But it is not, or should not be, teacher dominated - the pupil must be encouraged to say what she feels about the work she has been doing. So, profiling becomes a two-way communication process. But to be effective as such, both teacher and pupil must be clear about the criteria on which they are assessing, and to do so means that both should know the criteria - usually in advance of the work being done. The pupil will then understand what is considered important about the piece of work before she starts, and will become more skilful in deciding whether she is fulfilling the criteria as she goes along. The work becomes, not just something for which a teacher's mark is required, but a piece of work which is critically evaluated also by its owner, who takes responsibility for it. It is clear that assessment for the profile is an integral part of the curriculum, and as such it needs to be planned for and incorporated when the teacher is drawing up her schemes of work. The profile lends itself particularly to the modular approach to the curriculum as it can be designed to show the personal development which has taken place during a programme of work which might have stretched over a period of a few weeks. It is through this continuous nature of assessment as an integral part of the curriculum that teachers should be looking for a way forward in the management of time.

ASSESSMENT AND NEGOTIATION

Negotiation at its simplest level involves talking, listening, understanding and compromising. If no shift in position takes place, then negotiation has been unsuccessful. Negotiation can be seen to be a compromise worked at by people who genuinely want an agreed solution, or it could be seen, cynically, as one 'side' getting its own way by manipulating the other. Perhaps these two views represent the two extremes on a continuum of showing goodwill in negotiation, and in terms of negotiation in the classroom, the manipulative extreme might express the view 'you did this didn't you?', with which, as a leading statement, and depending on how it was delivered, the pupil would be loath to disagree, whereas the other extreme might ask 'can you describe what happened?' or 'can you tell me what you did?', leaving the way open for the pupil to reply as she wants to. It should be said, however that the manipulative extreme may not arise from ill intentions, but from a desire to complete the negotiation as swiftly as possible because of the pressure of time, or as a result of lack of skill or of lack of awareness of the style adopted by the negotiator; and, at the other extreme, openness will only be seen as genuine if the routine ethos of the classroom allows and encourages pupils to express their views. There is a concern that assessment and negotiation will be only at a superficial level unless or until trust has been established between the participants.

Negotiating is perhaps a rather strong word to use in connection with discussing children's work, as in these days it holds political overtones of major disagreements, unions, strikes and so on. It could be that this is one of the reasons why teachers shy away from the concept of negotiation, coupled with the fact that over many years, they have come to expect that what they say will be accepted as being correct and therefore needing no discussion on which compromises could be made. When looking at negotiation as a new idea with which the staff will have to become familiar, it should be remembered that teachers have always talked to pupils about their work, some teachers have talked more than others, and to some pupils more than others, but an element of negotiation has been developing quietly over the years. The differences in the negotiation needed for profiling are that the profiles themselves tend to structure the discussions to a certain extent, they perhaps ensure a fairer distribution of teacher attention to all pupils in the class, and they allow pupils to respond to the teacher's comments, which they have not been used to doing.

There are skills which we as teachers will need to develop if our discussions with pupils are to be meaningful, and these should be supported by INSET for the whole staff. They include the ability to open opportunities for pupils to talk, to listen to what they are saying, to show in non-verbal and verbal communication that we want to hear what they say, to help them to move their thinking forward without telling them what to think, and to assist them in setting their own targets for personal development. It is all too easy to fall into some of the mistaken responses outlined by Nelson-Jones (1983), a few of which are shown as follows: directing 'I think we should talk about this ...' judging 'your work is very messy, you know!' moralising 'you really should have a better attitude towards your work!' glibly reassuring, when there may be no justification for this 'yes, I know how you feel, but you'll be all right!' giving advice 'if I were you, I should ...', or 'why don't you...'.

Some of these responses will be familiar to many of us, as, trying to do our best, we clutch at straws amidst the stress caused by the noise of 30 other pupils, the lack of time and the lack of adequate training. This assumes however, that negotiation is only going on between the teacher and the pupil, and whilst there is an important place for this, there is also room for the negotiation which we have seen taking place during peer group assessment. Here the negotiation occurs between peers, but it can then be acknowledged by the teacher.

Another way of dealing with the problem of negotiation is through the way in which the assessment is structured. There is a range of different assessment procedures as we have seen, and of these, some are more likely to produce protracted negotiation than others. For instance, providing tests are carefully devised to assess specific cognitive objectives (bearing in mind what has been previously discussed about testing) - for instance, recall of methods of adding, subtracting, multiplying and dividing fractions - then the results could be assumed to reasonably reliably inform both pupil and teacher whether the pupil can remember how to do them, without the necessity of a great deal of negotiation. Expressive objectives however - those concerned with attitudes and feelings - more readily lend themselves to impressionistic assessment, whether the impression from the evidence available is formed by the child, the child's peers, or the teacher. All this is far more open to being a matter of opinion, and therefore, much more likely to need negotiation to take place. It might be prudent therefore, when drawing up profiles, to keep in mind the amount of time likely to be needed by both the assessment and the negotiation procedures, to balance these within the accepted philosophy of what we are trying to achieve, and to plan for them at appropriate stages in our schemes of work, which will be at intervals - though not necessarily regular intervals - during the year.

Finally let us deal with the problem of the child with whom we cannot negotiate an agreed assessment. To a certain extent, this could be a theoretical rather than a practical problem, as if the theory has been applied adequately to the construction of our profiles, our guidelines and evidence should be clear enough for there not to be too much discrepancy over cognitive objectives and criteria.

128

Where problems might be more likely to occur will be in the area of affective objectives - such as in use of time, putting effort into work, how the work looks, and so on - because it is here that the pupil will feel that she knows about her commitment and attitudes towards work, people and school, whereas she would think that her teachers and peers can only act as observers and interpret what they see of her behaviour. It is a matter of her opinion compared with theirs, and she may feel very justified that her opinion is the only one which is correct. Obviously she is entitled to hold her opinion, while the task of the teacher and peers would be to point out that although that is the way she sees things, they come across differently for this, that or the other reason - and cite the evidence. If there is still no movement of positions, nor reasonable likelihood of compromise, then either the assessment could be left blank, or, as one or two of our pupils suggested, both the teacher's and the pupil's opinion should be allowed to stand. This is where a useful aspect to profiling would be the opportunity at a Consultation Evening, for pupil, teacher and parent to discuss the profile together.

Perhaps we also need to consider that compromise is not always necessary, that people inevitably hold varying opinions of others, and that, depending on the perspective, the reality of a person's personality or abilities may seem very different to different people. When all is said and done, how can we be so sure that we are 'right' and that the person we are assessing is wrong, when it is impossible to know absolute truth in understanding the complexity of human beings. We will strive to explain our thoughts to our pupils, but our thoughts are merely our opinions, based on our values and beliefs, of reality as we see it.

Introducing profiling into our school has come to be intrinsically linked with the development of staff thinking and the extensive searching for solutions that will involve us in trying out ideas and evaluating their success, in being prepared to put a lot of effort into a long day's work, and in being prepared to change course if the theoretical and empirical experience combine to show a need for doing so.

Chapter Six

USING THE COMPUTER

As we were working from first principles in the design of our profiling forms in the sense that we created them to suit our particular purposes, we were greatly advantaged by being able to rely on our own computing resources to draw them up, thereby being able to amend them as and when we felt it was necessary. The early work on the progress reports, for instance, frequently involved changes in their lay out and wording. There was no difficulty in adjusting the original copy on the computer, and the fact that it was so simple to do meant that we did not feel restrained in making alterations, which we might have done otherwise. The same was true for the profiles, which were reproduced in the same format throughout from their original design saved on the computer disk, and we felt that the end result looked like a professional product, giving an air of authenticity to the project.

Once the profiles and report sheets were all designed, we looked for a way of using the computer to print out the completed Records of Achievement. We felt that the major purpose of profiling was in the work of teachers with children in the classroom, rather than in writing out a seemingly endless number of agreed statements, and we were very concerned that the weighty administration involved in recording achievement would quite quickly become its downfall. It has already been seen that many of the staff would be having to think through the demands of changing their teaching style and strategies in order to fulfil the profiling process expected of them, and to impose, also, a lengthier system of reporting, would have amounted to a failure to understand the additional workload they were carrying and to show consideration towards them.

The problem we were searching to overcome in using a computer to print out the summative documents was that for each skill, there would be a choice from two, three or four alternatives, and the time involved in using clerical help to type in the selected comments for each of 151 children would have been prohibitive, always supposing that there might have been someone available to do this - which, of course, there was not! The computer connection we were looking for was a software programme which would cope with 'if X = Y', then print Y', or, to use an example from the English profile, 'when you come to 'vocabulary skills' please select and print for this child, 'I know a wide variety of words and I can use a dictionary or thesaurus to help improve my vocabulary.'

I was delighted to find that such a programme did exist, and that, by feeding in the relevant information, such as the criteria for the skills in each subject, and then drawing up a text which looked like a string of complicated hieroglyphics, the software would merge the criteria selected into a free flowing piece of text, the quality of which depends directly on the comments of the profile and the skill of the programmer. This is a sample of what can be done:

Art/pottery

When using her imagination, "PUPIL" "IF AS1="a1"" "INCLUDE a1""ENDIF""IF AS1="a2"""INCLUDE a2""ENDIF" "IF AS1="a3"""INCLUDE a3""ENDIF".

'AS1' represents Art Skills 1, which corresponds to 'Using information' (Table 6.1). The first of the comments is saved as 'a1' and is '... can usually think of one or two ideas of (her) own'; the second comment, 'a2' is '... can usually think of ideas', whilst the third, 'a3' reads '...has lots of ideas for (her) work'. So if 'AS1' is 'a1' on a child's profile, and the pupil's name is Jane, then the first sentence reads, 'When using her imagination, Jane can usually think of one or two ideas of her own'.

The background text needs to be built up gradually, and care has to be taken that the inserted comments - the assessment criteria of the skills - sound sensible when applied to the skeleton structure. For instance, in composing the text, account must be taken of the fact that any one of two, three or four comments could be inserted, so, each of these needs to be tried out for style and comprehension before proceeding further. In the example cited, each of the alternative comments fits in satisfactorily. Now, if it has not been done before when the profiles were originally being drafted by the departments, it is sensible to check at this stage for excessive repetition of words such as 'usually' or 'with help' or 'often', and to try to ensure that, assuming a run of same level comments, there will be a variety of words to describe what the pupil has been doing.

One way of doing this is to isolate the comments at the different levels, and to ensure that if a pupil does fall into the same category throughout, then the description of her achievements sounds varied and interesting, but also reflects the wording on the profile. If changes need to be made at this stage, they will also have to be made to the profile, as there should be no significant change in language - which might prejudice the intended meaning - as we move from one step to the next, the profile and record of achievement existing in a symbiotic-like relationship to each other. The mathematical skills will serve as an example of checking throughout the text:

level one
- can do some number work accurately
- can solve some problems, especially with help
- can remember one or two mathematical ideas
- likes to check that she is doing things the right way
- needs a lot of time to do things

level two
- can do most number work accurately
- can solve problems and does not often have to ask for help
- can remember some new mathematical ideas
- can follow instructions with only a little help
- can usually present work in an orderly way when she tries
- takes a lot of time before settling to work

level three
- works accurately using number rules
- most of the time can solve problems on her own

- can remember most new mathematical ideas
- can follow instructions on her own
- usually presents work in an orderly way
- mostly makes good use of time in lessons

On the whole these comments would fit together to make a fairly varied piece of prose. They could be criticised on the grounds that the words 'most', 'help' and 'on her own' appear too often, but as we need them to describe the criteria, we will have to content ourselves with the fact that they are reasonably well spread out. So the skeleton text (Table 6.2) is planned as is shown below:

When "Jane" is using the four rules of number, she "... skill 1 ..." and she can use these skills "... skill 2 ...". "Jane" can remember "... skill 3 ..." of the mathematical ideas covered during the year "... skill 4 ...". She "... skill 5 ...". "Jane" "... skill 6 ...".

Once the pupil's achievements are inserted, the text becomes understandable, as will be seen in the examples below. In order to keep the examples as clear as possible, each one represents only one level of skill, whereas in reality, it was our experience that most pupils achieved a variety of skill levels in their profiles. The words underlined are the comments which have been transferred from the profiles.

Level one: When Jenny is using the four rules of number, she can do some of this work accurately and she can use these skills to work out some problems, especially if given help. Jenny can remember one or two of the mathematical ideas covered during the year and likes to check that she's following instructions correctly. She finds it hard to set out her work in an orderly way. Jenny needs a lot of time to do things.

Level two: When Jem is using the four rules of number, she can do much of this work accurately and she can use these skills to work out problems without having to ask for much help. Jem can remember some of the mathematical ideas covered during the year and needs only a little help to follow written or spoken instructions correctly. She can usually present her work in an orderly way when she tries.

Jem takes a lot of time before settling to work.

Level three: When Sally is using the four rules of number, she works accurately and she can use these skills to work out most problems on her own. Sally can remember most of the mathematical ideas covered during the year and can follow written and spoken instructions on her own. She usually presents her work in an orderly way. Sally mostly makes good use of time in lessons.

The software is programmed to interpret "IF the skill is THIS, then INCLUDE THIS in the text". Readers experienced in using computers will probably appreciate that drawing up such a programme readily lends itself to human error, and that the practicalities of producing an error-free, working text are not without operational frustrations! I was alerted to one of the most common errors through the cryptic computer communication 'Missing ENDIF', which meant that the text could not select the appropriate statements. So I had to comb through the text to find where I had omitted to insert "ENDIF" which was sometimes difficult to see, until I became wise to the subtle difference between "ENDIF" and "END IF". Until the space between END and IF was spotted and corrected the programme would not run. I was advised of another error by the friendly computer communication 'Your IF statements are too deeply nested', which threw me into total confusion, and sent me back to review my skeleton text to see if I could discover what this meant before I could put it right. When I did work out what the computer was telling me, I could see how totally appropriate the comment was! If I had omitted the relevant sign to close the computer search for data in the middle of a lengthy run of instructions, then the 'IF' statements would be inadequately separated from each other and therefore, 'too deeply nested'!

The preparation for using the computer was a time-consuming business and needed meticulous attention to detail; the build up of the text had to be completed step by step, with each section being checked through systematically to ensure that the programme would run and that there would be no malfunctioning when we came to using it for printing out the summative documents.

The final form to be drawn up before we could

computerise our records of achievement was a profile proforma for each child, on which would be listed the skills for each subject, which the teacher would fill in as appropriate. Although this was not absolutely necessary, we felt that from an administrative point of view it would be quicker and more compact for the people who were going to key in the codes to have them tidily to hand, rather than spaced out through the many pages of subject profiles. The sequence of events then became:

- discuss and complete profiles in lessons
- subject teachers fill in proforma for each child
- codes are keyed into computer
- computer prints out final documents
- pupils read these in school, and then take home to parents.

Two examples of the final record of achievement are included in this chapter, and are taken from the 151 we printed in the summer term, the names having been changed to ensure anonymity. It should be pointed out, however, that only the subject-specific skills were computerised. The first page of the final record of achievement (Table 3.23) was completed by the form teacher by hand, in consultation with each child, and gave a clear picture of the personal qualities of the pupil such as punctuality and attendance, participation in school activities and those outside school, and the personal skills and attitudes which she wanted to have on her record.

The first example of a completed record of achievement (Table 6.3) recorded the following subject specific skills:

Name: Caroline West

English		mathematics		science	
	n1		m2		sc2
	n4		m5		sc5
	n7		m7		sc8
	n11		m10		sc11
	n13		m13		sc14
	n17		m19		sc16
			75%		23%
			57%		61%
			66%		

French		history	h5	geography	g2
does not take			h8		g4
French			h13		g7
			h16		g10
			10%		g13
			46%		g16
					g20
					g24

RE	re1	art	a1	home econ.	he2
	re5		a5		he5
RE	re7	art	a7	home econ.	he7
	re9		a11		he11
	re14		a14		he14
	re15		a18		he17
	re18				33%
	re21				63%
	32%				
	50%				

textiles	t2	music	mu1	phys. ed.	p12
	t5		mu8	discus & high jump	
	t8		mu9		p26
	t12				
	t15				
	t20				

The second example (Table 6.4) was drawn up from the following codes:

Name: Janice Jones

English	n3	mathematics	m3	science	sc2
	n6		m6		sc6
	n8		m9		sc8
	n11		m12		sc11
	n15		m16		sc14
	n18		m20		sc17
			85%		74%
			94%		61%
			66%		

French	f3	history	h4	geography	g3
	f6&7		h6		g6
	f10		h12		g9

	f16		h14		g12
French	f19	history	h18	geography	g14
	95%		60%		g18
	62%		46%		g21
					g24
RE	re3	art	a2	home econ.	he3
	re5		a5		he5
	re8		a8		he7
	re11		a12		he11
	re14		a15		he15
	re17		a18		he18
	re19				77%
	re23				63%
textiles	t2	music	mu4	phys. ed.	p13
	t3		mu8	shot and 100m	
	t7		mu12		p27
	t11				
	t15				
	t16				

Once the codes had been keyed into the computer, the programme operated speedily enough. The worst feature was inputting the codes, which, with 151 pupils having at least 90 codes each, was tedious and subject to human error, and any errors might have passed undetected. The input process would greatly benefit from a technology which would feed the codes directly into the computer to be processed and printed, without the need for further human intervention.

It will no doubt be noticed that the final part of the profiles - the pupil's statements of what had been enjoyed, and the plans for the future - were omitted from the computer version, although it had been intended to include them in the original handwritten document (Table 3.3). This omission was in the interests of operational ease and the limitations of time and was particularly unfortunate because it meant that some of the personal nature of the profile was lost in transfer, and also because the computer was starting to dictate what should be included in the final version of the document. This is not ultimately acceptable as the computer should be used as a tool to assist us rather than as a determinant of what we do or do not include, but, for this particular trial run, there simply was not enough time to have done anything differently.

Table 6.1: Art Skills

Date_____ 19____

Teacher_____ Name_____ Form_____

	pupil's opinion	teacher's opinion
USING IMAGINATION When we have to use our imagination		
A1 I can think of one or two ideas of my own		
A2 I can usually think of some ideas		
A3 I have lots of ideas for my work		
PRACTICAL SKILLS When we produce a piece of work in art		
A4 I know how I want my work to look		
A5 My drawing/painting looks something like I want it to		
A6 My pictures look as I want them to		
CREATIVITY When we make things from our ideas		
A7 I can make pictures but like quite a lot of help		
A8 I can make pictures and I need only a little help		
A9 I can work out and finish a project on my own		
TALKING When we talk about art work		
A10 I can talk a little about what I'm trying to do		
A11 I can tell another person what I'm trying to do		
A12 I like talking about my ideas		

Table 6.2: Computer programme (showing sample programme for mathematical skills)

"SET PUPIL=?ENTER PUPIL NAME?"
"SET SURNAME=?ENTER PUPIL SURNAME?"
"SET FORM=?ENTER PUPILS FORM?"
"SET NW1=?ENTER NUMBER WORK 1 MARK?"
"SET NW2=?ENTER NUMBER WORK 2 MARK?"
"SET NW3=?ENTER NW REMEMBERING FACTS 3 MARK?"
"SET NW4=?ENTER NW FOLLOWING INSTRUCTIONS 4 MARK?"
"SET NW5=?ENTER NW PRESENTATION OF WORK 5 MARK?"
"SET NW6=?ENTER NW USING TIME 6 MARK?"

"PUPIL" "SURNAME"   "FORM"

MATHEMATICS
When "PUPIL" is using the four rules of number, she "IF NW1="m1"""INCLUDE m1""ENDIF""IF NW1="m2"" "INCLUDE m2""ENDIF""IF NW1="m3"""INCLUDE m3""END IF"and she can use these skills "IF NW2="m4"""INCLUDE m4""ENDIF""IF NW2="m5"""INCLUDE m5""ENDIF""IF NW2=m6"""INCLUDE m6""ENDIF"
"PUPIL" can remember "IF NW3="m7"""INCLUDE m7" "ENDIF""IF NW3="m8"""INCLUDEm8""ENDIF""IF NW3 ="m9"""INCLUDE m9""ENDIF" of the mathematical ideas covered during the year "IF NW4="m10a"""INCLUDE m10a""ENDIF""IF NW4="m10b"""INCLUDE m10b""ENDIF" "IF NW4="m11"""INCLUDE m11""ENDIF""IF NW4="m12"" "INCLUDE m12""ENDIF". She "IF NW5="m13"""INCLUDE m13""ENDIF""IF NW5="m14"""INCLUDE m14""ENDIF""IF NW5="m15"""INCLUDE m15""ENDIF""IF NW5="m16" ""INCLUDE m16""ENDIF". "PUPIL" "IF NW6="m17"" "INCLUDE m17""ENDIF""IF NW6="m18"""INCLUDE m18" "ENDIF""IF NW6="m17 and m18""INCLUDE m17andm18" "ENDIF""IF NW6="m19"""INCLUDE m19""ENDIF""IF NW6= "m17andm19"""INCLUDE m17andm19""ENDIF""IF NW6= "m20"""INCLUDE m20""ENDIF"

Table 6.3: Completed Record of Achievement 1

Caroline West   1W

Caroline has discussed her year's work with her teachers and the following is a record of some of her skills and achievements at the present time.

ENGLISH
When using her imagination to write stories and poems, she has a few ideas. She can write some of these down. Caroline knows and can understand words which we come across often. In her own reading she can choose a book and read it to herself. She can read aloud to a small group of her friends. In discussion or drama lessons, Caroline can say what she thinks to a small group.

MATHEMATICS
When Caroline is using the four rules of number, she can do much of this work accurately and she can use these skills to work out problems without having to ask for much help. Caroline can remember one or two of the mathematical ideas covered during the year and likes to check that she's following instructions correctly. She finds it hard to present her work in an orderly way. Caroline mostly makes good use of time in lessons.

Her aural test was 75%. Her examination result was 57% and the examination average for the year group was 66%.

SCIENCE
Caroline can usually follow instructions by herself and when working in the laboratory, she can follow the safety rules but sometimes needs reminding of them. When looking at living things, pictures and diagrams, she usually notices a few things of importance about them. Caroline can usually think of some ideas and finds some of her solutions to problems work well. Caroline can write an account of her science work if someone helps her.

Her test result was 23% and the test average for the year group was 61%.

HISTORY
When imagining what it was like to be an Anglo Saxon, Caroline can think of a few details about what life was like then. Caroline understands why we need historical evidence to find out about the past. She can remember some of the things she has learnt about the Anglo Saxons. Unfortunately she finds it difficult to do her work neatly.

Her examination result was 10% and the examination average for the year group was 46%.

GEOGRAPHY
Caroline can usually draw plans to scale and if given help, she can work with graphs, plotting information. She can find things on an ordnance survey map if someone helps her and can use an atlas to find a few of the following: continents, countries, seas, rivers, mountains and so on. When describing places, she needs to use her own words, rather than geographical terms. She finds writing and drawing difficult to do neatly. Caroline can remember some of the signs, symbols, geographical words and other information which she has learnt. She mostly makes good use of time in lessons.

RELIGIOUS EDUCATION
Caroline can draw maps with some help and can also use them to find places mentioned in the Bible, by herself. When cutting, pasting and putting things together to make masks, posters and so on, Caroline is able to make her models look something like she wants them to. Unfortunately she finds it difficult to do her work neatly. She can find references in the Bible on her own and can remember some of the things she has learnt during the year. Caroline knows what she wants to say in discussion but does not always say it. She needs a lot of time to do things.

Her examination result was 31% and the year average was 50%.

ART/POTTERY
When using her imagination, Caroline can think of one or two ideas of her own, and in producing a piece of work, she can make it look something like she wants it to. She can use her ideas to make things, but likes quite a lot of help.

Caroline can tell another person what she is trying to do and can follow instructions needing only a little help to do so. She mostly makes good use of time in lessons.

HOME ECONOMICS
In organising her work in the kitchen Caroline can usually think out what to do next and frequently is able to pick out and use the equipment she needs, without help. She can usually manage to use the cooker on her own. Caroline mostly makes good use of time in lessons. She can remember some of the things which she has learnt this year and can follow written or spoken instructions if given one or two reminders.

Her test result was 33% and the average for the year was 63%.

TEXTILES
Caroline can set up the sewing machine on her own and can dial a pattern and machine accurately and confidently. When handsewing, she can work several stitches accurately. She can make an attractive design using colour and shape, and can suggest ideas for stitches. Caroline can follow instructions with only a little help. She has a strong sense of personal motivation.

MUSIC
Caroline can clap the rhythms to tunes made up by the class. When making up music in groups, she enjoys playing the music on the instruments. Caroline can remember some of the instruments of the orchestra.

PHYSICAL EDUCATION
The rounders skills taught this term include throwing, catching, running, fielding, hitting the ball and bowling. Caroline can do some of these, some of the time. Her best events in athletics so far this term (June 24th) have been discus and high jump. She can swim some distance in a fairly good style.

Table 6.4: Completed Record of Achievement 2

Janice Jones   1K

Janice has discussed her year's work with her teachers and the following is a record of some of her skills and achievements at the present time.

ENGLISH

When using her imagination to write stories and poems, she has lots of ideas which she can write about confidently. She can write down her ideas carefully, paying attention to spelling and punctuation rules. Janice knows quite a lot of words, and can use her dictionary to help her find those that she does not know. In her own reading she can choose a book and can read it to herself. She can read clearly and with expression to the class. In discussion or drama lessons, Janice takes part and enjoys expressing her ideas to other people.

MATHEMATICS

When Janice is using the four rules of number, she works accurately and she can use these skills to work out most problems on her own. Janice can remember most of the mathematical ideas covered during the year and can follow written or spoken instructions on her own. She can organise and present her work in an orderly manner. Janice has a strong sense of personal motivation.

Her aural test result was 85%. Her examination result was 94% and the examination average for the year group was 66%.

SCIENCE

Janice can usually follow instructions by herself and when working in the laboratory, she follows the safety rules carefully at all times. When looking at living things, pictures and diagrams, she usually notices a few things of importance about them. Janice can usually think of some ideas and finds some of her solutions to problems work well. Janice can write an account of her science work without help.

FRENCH

When listening to simple French being spoken, Janice can understand most of it. She can use 'être' and more complicated verbs correctly and can always understand the French passages she reads. Janice can describe the weather and seasons in French very well and can write French correctly. Her examination result was 95% and the average for the year was 62%.

HISTORY

Janice can draw a timeline of her life, placing events in the correct order. She can also use a timeline to show the difference between AD and BC. When imagining what it was like to be an Anglo Saxon, she can describe how they punished criminals, carried out trial by ordeal, and buried their dead. Janice understands why we need historical evidence to find out about the past and can usually tell the difference between primary and secondary sources. She can remember quite a few things she has learnt about the Anglo Saxons. She does her work neatly.

Her examination result was 60% and the examination average for the year group was 46%.

GEOGRAPHY

Janice can draw plans and sketch maps accurately and can work with graphs, plotting and interpreting information. She can read and get information from ordnance survey maps and can use an atlas to find continents, countries, seas, oceans, rivers, mountains and so on, and can also use the key and index. When describing places, she can use some geographical words correctly. She usually works neatly. Janice can remember most of the signs, symbols, geographical words and other information which she has learnt. She mostly makes good use of time in lessons.

RELIGIOUS EDUCATION

Janice can draw maps on her own and can also use maps to find places mentioned in the Bible, by herself. When cutting, pasting and putting things together to make masks, posters and so on, Janice is able to do this on her own, with pleasing results. She always does her work neatly. She can find references in the Bible on her own and has a good memory for a wide range of facts. Janice usually takes part in discussion and says what she thinks. She mostly makes good use of time in lessons.

ART/POTTERY
When using her imagination, Janice can usually think of ideas, and in producing a piece of work, she can make it look something like she wants it to. She can use her ideas to make things, and needs only a little help. Janice likes talking about her ideas and can follow instructions on her own. She mostly makes good use of time in lessons.

HOME ECONOMICS
In organising her work in the kitchen Janice can cope confidently and frequently is able to pick out and use the equipment she needs, without help. She can usually manage to use the cooker on her own. Janice mostly makes good use of time in lessons. She can remember most of the things she has learnt this year and can follow written or spoken instructions without needing to be reminded.

TEXTILES
Janice can set up the sewing machine on her own and can machine if given some help. When hand sewing, she can work some different stitches fairly neatly. She can make up a design using colour and shape on her own. Janice can follow instructions with only a little help. She takes a lot of time before settling to work.

MUSIC
Janice can play the rhythms and notes on the recorder to tunes made up by the class. When making up music in groups, she enjoys playing the music on the instruments. Janice can recognise the different sounds of the instruments of the orchestra and understands how they are made.

PHYSICAL EDUCATION
The rounders skills taught this term include throwing, catching, running, fielding, hitting the ball and bowling. Janice can often manage these well. Her best events in

athletics so far this term (June 24th) have been shot and 100m. She can swim at least twenty lengths non-stop using good style and a range of strokes.

Chapter Seven

EXPERIENCES OF THE MATHEMATICS DEPARTMENT

In order to understand how profiling and recording achievement developed within the school, it is helpful to follow through the experiences of one particular department. Whilst each individual department will have coped with problems and processes which were idiosyncratic to the subject, the teachers' attitudes and beliefs, and the interdepartmental relationships, there are useful generalisations of experience which can be made from hearing about one particular case study.

At the beginning of the academic year 1986-7 the mathematics department had embarked on innovating the School Mathematics Project 11-16 for First Year pupils, following extensive discussion and INSET over the previous year. The department had been supported by the Advisory Teacher for mathematics in the Borough whose brief was to help the High Schools to implement the Cockroft approach to learning mathematics (Cockroft Report, 1982) and members of staff had been open to change in the pedagogical delivery of the mathematical curriculum particularly because they had encountered so many problems in the teaching of mixed ability groups - problems ranging from motivating the low attainers whilst still extending the able pupil, to maintaining the interest and individual momentum of all those who fell between these two extremes and at the same time giving adequate individual attention to each person.

With the arrival of SMP, three out of five lessons each week were devoted to using the SMP booklets, and in the other two the pupils followed a teacher-directed course in four main areas - decimals, angles, coordinates and sets and venn diagrams.

Much thought was applied to the skills the department should assess for their profile, taking into consideration the wide range of work which was being undertaken during the year. The other important issue in the profiling process, that of negotiation, was also explored fairly early in the year, when, just before the First Year Parents' Consultation Evening in November 1986, most of the pupils were asked to complete a general evaluation of their work to date, which formed the basis of a brief, individual discussion between teacher and pupil. This introduced a rudimentary form of negotiation, which has been discussed in greater detail in chapter two.

When considering drawing up a mathematics profile, the department had two main objectives in view. One was that the profile should encourage the pupil to think about her own learning, and the other was that a positive record of achievement should be built up as the result of the profiling process. It was hoped that this would be in a form which was interesting, clear, and informative for parents to read.

The department's first attempt at a full profile is shown in Table 7.1. The profile was divided into subject-specific skills - number, space, algebra, graphs and statistics; cross-curricular - information handling, problem solving, and physical motor skills; and personal and social skills and qualities. It was felt that this constituted a detailed account of what the pupil had done during the course of the year, and as such, would give the parent valuable information on a summative record of achievement. Table 7.2, was intended as an improvement on Table 7.1, with the information presented in a different way, and allowing space for the teacher's and the pupil's opinion, thereby giving a structured opportunity for some discussion to take place. At this stage, there was no clear plan as to how the profile would be offered to parents.

There followed considerable discussion on the format of the profile and of its very specific content, which it was felt relied too heavily on test results, thereby stressing outcomes rather than processes. The non-subject-specific skills began to look both extensive from the point of view of assessing them, and difficult to define in terms of a First Year pupil's experience. It was not clear exactly what was meant by some of the statements, albeit they sounded impressive. For instance, what type of 'complex instructions' would be given to a First Year pupil? What is meant by 'analysing problems' and if a pupil can analyse problems, does that automatically mean that she can solve them as well, as is implied in the comment bank? What constitutes a 'good' level of coordination in the use of ruler and compasses, and again, if a pupil can coordinate one, does that automatically mean she can coordinate the other as well?

By the beginning of the Spring Term, 1987, the organisation and format of other departmental profiles had begun to take shape. They were all much more general than the one drawn up by the mathematics department, so to remain in keeping with the others, and because it was felt that the detail stressed SMP work at the expense of the rest of the year's course work, it was decided to abandon the early models and to draw up the profile shown in Table 7.3.

Having consulted with others in the department, the teacher with special responsibility for First Year work felt that the skills identified covered a range of those which she wanted to assess, that they were appropriately worded for First Year pupils to understand, that the balance of cross-curricular, and subject-specific skills together with a more open space for the pupil to record work with which she was well pleased, allowed for all children to show positive aspects of their mathematical experiences, even if their level of attainment was low. The examination result would probably reveal the relative strength of the pupil at mathematics in comparison with the year group and it was thought that, despite the move towards criterion-referenced differentiation for GCSE, parental expectation might still demand this kind of comparative information at our particular school.

Following the whole staff INSET, described in chapters four and five, the mathematics department met to establish both each teacher's understanding of their profile's skills and comments, and also how they would set about putting the process into operation during the summer term. Three main problems presented themselves; the need to gather evidence of level of skills; the need for time to assess and negotiate; and the need to provide satisfying work with which the class could get on whilst this process was taking place.

As far as evidence of accuracy was concerned, it was decided that this should be tested through a series of addition, subtraction, multiplication and division sums which were mechanical in nature and did not demand the necessity to solve problems as well. Thus M1, M2 and M3 were to be decided on set criteria common to all the department. The second section - on working out problems - was more subjective and would rely on the relative amount of help which had been given during lessons throughout the year. 'Remembering facts' was to be based on marks achieved in course work tests, with the department agreeing percentage categories for each statement. The 'number work' and 'remembering facts' sections would be assessed on an individual basis, with considerable departmental direction based on test results being given in order to guide pupils into appropriate categories. It was thought that there would not be too much negotiation needed with these skills as they were considered to be fairly straightforward.

The three cross-curricular skills, included particularly to assess a general approach to work, were to be subjected to self and peer group assessment if the teacher was happy with this method of working. Members of staff in the department were asked to think about and record an assessment of each child in their mark books and compare this with the comment at which the children arrived through their group discussions. In the event, it was probably an unnecessary addition to the work load for the teachers to assess these skills separately, as it became apparent that it was more satisfying for pupil and teacher alike for the assessments to be made, discussed and agreed at the same time. Taking away the profile and completing it independently rather invalidated the feeling of cooperation generated by group/pupil/teacher discussion.

Peer group assessment was based on the evidence which pupils and their friends remembered from previous lessons or from looking through their books. Before they started to discuss the skills, each group was asked to think about what was meant by the statements and to feed back their thoughts to the class group. In that way, some standardisation of the meaning of the skills was achieved.

The section on 'following instructions' gave rise to a discussion between the staff on the type of instructions which should be considered, and it was agreed that the teacher's verbal instructions, together with the instructions in the booklets, such as 'Copy and complete this temperature graph', or 'Measure accurately the length of each animal and record it in your table', should be included. 'Presentation of work' was to be assessed by looking at the pupils' books, and the stress here was on orderliness as opposed to neatness, as it was felt that to work effectively in mathematics it was necessary to think in an orderly manner, whereas, although it was nice to see neat work, this did not always guarantee that the pupil had proceeded in logical steps to a conclusion. The section on 'use of time' was not intended to be hierarchical in nature. The first statement was not seen as pejorative in the sense that it is wrong to take a lot of time over things; it was intended merely as a statement of fact. The next comment about taking time before settling to work was covertly judgemental; the following two statements were close in meaning, but it was the experience of some members of staff that children could distinguish clearly between them and described 'personal motivation' as 'coming in the room, getting your books out and starting work without stopping to talk to other people or being distracted by whatever else was going on'. Other teachers thought that this statement was too difficult for the children to understand.

Once an agreed understanding had been reached amongst departmental staff, the teachers then discussed with their classes the meaning of the statements and gave guidance as to where the girls should look for evidence of the skills. The pupils were asked to think about and assess themselves individually as a preliminary to group assessment. When peer group assessment followed, they were told that they could not own a comment as appropriate for them if other members of the group disagreed with their opinion. It was at this stage that discussion took place, with the objective of changing opinions through looking at the evidence and discussing incidents which they could all remember. The tick in the box could only be made when everyone in the group agreed that the comment was relevant for that particular person. If, despite discussion, there was still disagreement, the teacher was called in to arbitrate. For the rest of the time, she would be moving discreetly around the room, listening for any problems and interceding if necessary, agreeing with group assessments where appropriate, and ticking the completed boxes.

Not all members of the mathematics department felt comfortable with this way of working, so each teacher followed her own personal preference in undertaking the profiling process. However, each of them began in the same way, using a class lesson in order to establish meanings, and dealing on an individual basis with 'number work' and 'remembering facts'. The teachers then collected in the profiles from the girls and went through them in their own time, returning them to the pupils in a session where final statements for 'number work' and 'remembering facts' were negotiated with each pupil individually. Following this, some of the department opted for peer group assessment with the final three skills, and although initially apprehensive about the level of noise, and whether the pupils would be fair with each other, eventually they felt much was gained in the discussions. The main points to emerge from peer group assessment were that the girls felt less embarrassed if a friend described their behaviour than if a member of staff did so; that many of the girls were very honest about themselves ('I quite often find myself looking out of the window instead of working' or 'It depends if L... is sitting next to me. If she is, I get distracted easily by her and start talking ...'); that the girls felt qualified to comment on each other's working habits, as quite often their friend's behaviour impinged on their ability to concentrate; that they felt they might know better than the teacher whether they or their friend had been working as they were closer to them and could see what was going on; and that on the whole, they discussed sensibly, citing evidence, rather than indulging in 'You do' - 'No I don't' arguments.

The department had identified as a problem the availability of time to complete the profiling process; the staff were also concerned about whether the rest of the class would be profitably employed whilst negotiation was taking place. As this work was undertaken just before the summer examinations a series of revision sheets was devised and it was intended that pupils should be able to work from these on their own. In the event, they asked a friend if they needed help, and this proved a fairly satisfactory arrangement, although the use of revision sheets was better sustained over a short period of time only. Some teachers used the SMP booklets and found their classes worked well without asking for help on those occasions. On average, five 40 minute lessons were used to negotiate with a class of 31; so, for that amount of time the teacher was not in a position to deal with queries from the class.

EVALUATION OF MATHEMATICS SKILLS AND LEVELS OF ATTAINMENT

Responses to the evaluation of the First Year profile from the department showed that the staff felt that the three subject-specific-skills and three cross-curricular skills seemed to be a manageable number with which to cope. Opinions were divided on the appropriateness of the differentiation of levels of skills but all members were agreed on the need for advice and for the opportunity to talk through with others in the department as to how they would set about improving these for next year. The need for INSET on negotiation skills was also identified.

Most of the department felt that completing the profiles gave a valuable opportunity for the girls to stop and think about the work they had done and the way in which they had worked; it was felt that for some girls the discussion would have increased their confidence in themselves as they realised that their teacher or the other girls had a higher opinion of them than they themselves did; and the development of the relationship with individual members of staff was seen as an advantage, in that it enabled girls to give voice to their opinions, and to explain to the teacher how they felt about their achievements and their aims for the future. It provided a structured opportunity for self assessment and educational counselling.

One of the main disadvantages was seen to be the amount of time taken over the negotiation, and the difficulty in sustaining class lessons whilst this process was going on. Certainly the individualised learning through the SMP booklets was of value here; the revision sheets were also of some value. The problems with the revision sheets were the variation in the speed at which each pupil worked - with the resultant 'I've finished this sheet, which one shall I do next?'; giving out the answers; and providing help if necessary - which it was on occasions.

Much of this evaluation has been arrived at through the fairly structured process of questionnaire and informal interview, as described in the next chapter, but of significant value also has been informal discussion between members of staff. The problems we have enountered are not easy ones to solve, but there are certain alternative approaches which would improve our practice for next year, which are organisational in nature and which can be incorporated without requiring major change in policy or input through INSET for instance. Specifically the process might be improved if some of the comments for the skills were re-worded, and if the profiling were spread throughout the year - which had always been intended, but by introducing it at a particular point in time in order to present a different type of end of year report, the initial time scale was inevitably unsatisfactory.

Spreading the profiling throughout the year is particularly important as it is the process which should be stressed rather than an end of year, 'bolted-on' product. The process is significant because it is through reviewing progress as the year goes by that the pupils will be able to adapt their behaviour and practices according to what they discover about themselves. To become aware of unsatisfactory practices only at the end of the year is no great improvement on finding these out from traditional style reports, apart from certain advantages accruing from the democratisation of the process. It is through the ongoing nature of the formative process of profiling that pupils will become increasingly aware of their strengths and weaknesses; this involvement in assessing themselves should lead them on to setting targets, and to become more motivated to improve their skills and attitudes. Spreading the profiling through the year would also ameliorate the time factor, in that it would break up the amount of talking which needed to be done at any one time on an individual basis between teacher and child.

The other improvement the mathematics department can introduce for next year is to change some of the comments which describe the skills they have identified. Anyone who has been involved in drawing up such comments will know that it is a thankless task, in that it is so easy for outsiders to look at them and proclaim them to be virtually meaningless in both their simplicity and generality. All comments in profiles should be worded so that they can be readily understood by anyone who might use them; in particular at First Year level, the use of language is crucial to the understanding of the participants for whom they have been designed. Not only should the language be scrutinised for degree of difficulty, but also, it is often only when a teacher comes to work with a class that ambiguities in what is actually meant become apparent and these need to be ironed out when recent experiences are reviewed. Although certain universal principles of profiling apply in widely differing institutions, it would seem that the wording of statements should be largely individual to each school, and depends for its effectiveness on teachers probing in depth what they want to say about skill levels, and revising their comment banks until they are satisfied that the statements really represent in words the meanings they have in mind.

This may sound simplistic, but is one of the most time consuming and difficult processes which need to be engaged in before a viable profile can be produced.

REVIEWING THE MATHEMATICS PROFILE

With these thoughts in mind, the mathematics department met together at the end of the summer term 1987 to analyse and improve their skill statements and comment banks. The staff systematically went through each of the skills and discussed the problems they had encountered in using them. It was felt that 'accuracy in number work' was too vague, but that such a skill was important and the assessment of it should be used as a diagnostic tool early on in the school year. The staff thought that testing in the four rules of number and then conflating the results into a generalised comment such as 'she can do most of this work accurately', detracted from the value of finding out any problems the child might have with these mathematical processes, and striving to remedy incorrect procedures. In other words, we had taken away an opportunity for specific target setting through generalisation, and as this was seen to be unsatisfactory, we looked for a way of expressing what the child 'can do' relative to accurate computation which would show also where any weaknesses lay.

The following format was decided upon:

NUMBER WORK
Working accurately
(you should have scored at least 9 out of 10 on your tests)

M1 I can add accurately
M2 I can subtract accurately
M3 I can multiply accurately
M4 I can divide accurately

The pupil could record her score in the appropriate box, and date it to enable a series of assessments to be recorded during the year.

The department discussed the section on problem solving at length, and found it hard to reach a consensus on improving it. As it stood, 'using the four rules of number to work out some problems' was too vague to be useful, and additionally the comment bank implied that it was good for the pupils not to ask for help. It was not made explicit from whom the help came - whether from the teacher, or other pupils, and it could also be the case that some girls should come and ask for help more often than they actually did. The section was thought to be too subjective and the evidence sufficiently controversial as to give rise to difficulties in discussion with the girls, so for the time being a decision was taken to abandon it.

'Remembering facts' had proved to be acceptable, but to make absolutely clear what was being assessed, it was agreed to alter the title to 'remembering facts for tests' and to include appropriate boxes for percentages to be written in as evidence. Pupil and teacher between them would have to negotiate the level of skill to be designated in the summative document, based on the record of test results.

There was much discussion on 'following instructions'. On the one hand, it was thought to be an important section, but on the other, the distinction between which instructions were to be followed was not clear. There was a need for the department to explore in some depth the type of instruction which held significance for them; it seemed that for some teachers the instructions assumed more importance than for others. One teacher for instance, described what she meant quite vividly. She said,

> I ask them to lead in quietly and stand at their place without talking. They get inside and stand talking amongst themselves. I tell them to stop talking. Eventually they do. I tell them to sit down and get out their exercise books, put the date and write classwork at the start of their work. I go round and find that some have written what I have asked them to write and others have not. I ask them to put down their pens whilst I talk to them. Some do and some do not. These are the sort of instructions I mean when I ask them to assess whether they follow instructions. I think they should be able to do these things without the instruction having to be repeated over and over again.

Another teacher agreed and mentioned that the department had drawn up a system for the children to mark and organise their work. Some girls adhered to the instructions for doing this and others did not. As the instructions were important to the organisation of the individualised learning scheme, it was thought that the girls needed to be aware of the significance in following instructions, thereby taking a real responsibility for their own learning. After much talking around the subject, the staff decided to use two statements only for the 'following instructions' section, one of which was a negative one, which would be used only in the formative process. When it came to recording achievements for parents to see, if the comment were positive it would be included, but if it were not, then it would be left out altogether - but at least it would have formed the subject of discussion between teacher and pupil and was therefore amenable to target setting and improvement.

'Presentation of work' was dealt with relatively swiftly. M13 - 'I find it hard to set out my work in an orderly way' - had proved to be a useful category, but 'I can usually present my work in an orderly way when I try' allowed too generous an interpretation to be made. What the staff wanted to say was that this pupil should make more consistent efforts to try harder to present work in an orderly manner. The statement was reworded as 'I present my work in an orderly way if I try', thereby allowing the interpretation that the pupil only achieves this if she tries, and the implication might be that she does not always try hard enough. It was thought that there did not exist a clear enough distinction between M15 and M16, so 'I usually do present my work in an orderly way' was deleted in favour of 'I organise and present my work in an orderly manner.'

In 'using time', M20 - 'I have a strong sense of personal motivation' - was not liked because some staff felt that pupils did not understand it sufficiently well and also that it was not substantially different from M19 - 'I mostly make good use of time in lessons' - which was preferred. Thus M20 was deleted, and 'mostly' was removed from M19. Two additional statements were agreed - 'I need a lot of time to do things but make good use of it in lessons' and, for those who find it hard to keep working for a whole lesson - 'I settle to work quickly, but lose concentration easily'.

At the same time as work was done on statements, the timing of the profiles was also revised. 'Number work' would be done as a diagnosis of numeracy problems early in the autumn term and repeated in the spring term. 'Remembering facts' could be completed as the tests were done during the course of the year and the other three sections - cross-curricular skills of 'following instructions', presentation of work' and 'using time' would be looked at by half term in the autumn term and again in early summer. It was thought that an early awareness of behaviour patterns and setting of targets should result in helping children to improve their learning. The department agreed that this process of cross-curricular profiling, probably using self and peer group assessment, should be completed within a single, or at most, a double lesson.

The revised profile may be seen in Table 7.4. The apparently simplistic task of rewording comment banks took over two hours, and involved the teachers in considerable discussion about the minutiae of exactly what was understood and what they really meant to say. One of them summed up their endeavours by saying, 'It's so frustrating. I know exactly what I want to say, but if I have to use just a few simple words, I can't seem to say it!' It was clear that the economic and accurate use of words was vital for the profiles to be satisfactory to the staff, but also that, until discussed, the same simple words could still mean different things to different people. It is reasonable to suppose that, despite the efforts made to produce comments which would hold unique meaning for our pupils and staff, there would be variations in individual understanding. It should be remembered, however, that one of the intrinsic values of profiling lies not so much in sifting children into the 'right' categories, but in the process of enabling the learner to stand aside, so that she might review all that has been accomplished, might perceive some of what still has to be done and as a result, will make a commitment towards achieving the targets she sets herself. It is only if this step is taken that the learner can be said to be taking responsibility for her own learning, which is a primary objective of the profiling process.

Table 7.1: Mathematics Record of Achievement 1

_____ 1986

Name _____ Form _____

Mathematical skills	best result	
Number a) can cope with addition, subtraction, multiplication and division of numbers	title	%
b) understands addition, subtraction, multiplication and division of decimals		
c) can use a simple calculator		
d) is skillful at using simple ratios		
e) is becoming used to number puzzles and patterns		
Space a) can fit simple shapes		
b) is becoming skillful at using rulers, compasses, angle measurers		
c) understands the use of grids, right and left directions		
d) has experienced working in three dimensions		
e) can cope with angles and degree of turning		
Algebra a) has experience of using negative numbers		
b) has worked at discovering rules		
c) is able to balance equations		
Graphs a) has worked at		
Statistics a) has worked at frequency tables and graphs to express data		

Table 7.1: continued

Cross-curricular skills

Information handling

Can present neat work	Frequently presents work well
Can remember basic facts	Has a good memory for a wide range of facts
Can follow simple instructions if guided	Can follow complex instructions independently

Problem solving skills

Can understand simple problems	Shows ability in tackling mathematical problems
Sometimes misreads problems and finds difficulty in solving them	Analyses problems systematically and can use necessary skills for solving them
Finds it difficult to understand data presented in tables	Is able to deal with data presented in tables independently

Physical motor skills

Finds using rulers/compasses hard	Has good level of coordination in use of ruler/compasses

Personal and social qualities

Takes a lot of time settling down to work	Can organise herself to make good use of time
Needs encouragement to start work	Enjoys working independently
Teacher's attention often drawn to behaviour	Does not often have to be disciplined by the teacher
Prefers to work on own than working together with others	Works cooperatively in 2s or a group

Table 7.2: Mathematics Record of Achievement 2

_____ 1986

Name _____ Form _____

Mathematical skills	best result	
	title	%
Number		
a) can cope with addition, subtraction, multiplication and division of numbers		
b) understands addition, subtraction, multiplication and division of decimals		
c) can use a simple calculator		
d) is skillful at using simple ratios		
e) is becoming used to number puzzles and patterns		
Space		
a) can fit simple shapes		
b) is becoming skillful at using rulers, compasses, angle measurers		
c) understands the use of grids, right and left directions		
d) has experienced working in three dimensions		
e) can cope with angles and degree of turning		
Algebra		
a) has experience of using negative numbers		
b) has worked at discovering rules		
c) is able to balance equations		
Graphs		
a) has worked at		
Statistics		
a) has worked at frequency tables and graphs to express data		

Table 7.2: continued

Cross-curricular skills

teacher's opinion	pupil's opinion	Information handling
		A1 Can present neat work
		A2 Frequently presents work well
		A3 Finds difficulty in remembering basic facts
		A4 Can remember basic facts
		A5 Has a good memory for a wide range of facts
		A6 Can follow simple instructions if guided
		A7 Can follow simple instructions
		A8 Can follow complex instructions independently

teacher's opinion	pupil's opinion	Problem solving skills
		B1 Sometimes has difficulty in reading problems
		B2 Can understand simple problems
		B3 Can analyse and solve problems by herself
		B4 Finds it difficult to understand data in tables
		B5 Is able to read and use data in tables by herself

Table 7.2: continued

Physical motor skills

teacher's opinion	pupil's opinion	
		C1 Finds using rulers/compasses hard
		C2 Has good level of coordination in use of ruler/compasses

Personal and social qualities

teacher's opinion	pupil's opinion	
		D1 Takes a lot of time settling down to work
		D2 Can organise herself to make good use of time
		D3 Needs encouragement to start work
		D4 Enjoys working independently
		D5 Teacher's attention often drawn to her behaviour
		D6 Does not often have to be disciplined by the teacher
		D7 Prefers to work on own rather than with others
		D8 Works cooperatively in 2s or a group

163

Table 7.3: Mathematics Skills 1

Date_____ 19____

Teacher_____ Name_____ Form_____

NUMBER WORK When we work at adding, taking away, multiplying and dividing	pupil's opinion	teacher's opinion
M1 I can do some of this work accurately		
M2 I can do most of this work accurately		
M3 I work accurately		
When we use these skills to work out some problems		
M4 I can do some of them, especially if given help		
M5 I can do this, and do not often have to ask for help		
M6 Most of the time I can do this on my own		
REMEMBERING FACTS When we have to remember new mathematical ideas		
M7 I can remember one or two of them		
M8 I can remember some of them		
M9 I can remember most of them		
FOLLOWING INSTRUCTIONS When we have to follow simple written or spoken instructions		
M10 I like to check that I'm doing it right		
M11 I only need a little help		
M12 I can do this on my own		

Table 7.3: continued

Name_____

	pupil's opinion	teacher's opinion
PRESENTATION OF WORK		
M13 I find it hard to set out my work in an orderly way		
M14 I can usually present my work in an orderly way when I try		
M15 I usually do present my work in an orderly way		
M16 I can organise and present my work in an orderly manner		
USING TIME		
M17 I need a lot of time to do things		
M18 I take a lot of time before settling to work		
M19 I mostly make good use of time in lessons		
M20 I have a strong sense of personal motivation		

The pieces of work I did especially well this year were

....

....

Next year I should like to improve..............................

My aural test result was ....%

My examination result was ....% and the examination

average for the year group was ....%.

Signed..

Table 7.4: Mathematics Skills 2

Date _____ 19___

Teacher _____ Name _____ Form _____

NUMBER WORK
When we do our number work
(You should have gained at least
9 out of 10)

	DATE		
M1 I can add accurately			
M2 I can subtract accurately			
M3 I can multiply accurately			
M4 I can divide accurately			

REMEMBERING FACTS
FOR TESTS
When we have to remember
new mathematical ideas

	DECIMALS	ANGLES	SETS AND VENN DIAGRAMS	COORDINATES	AGREED
M5 I can remember one or two of them (under 40%)					
M6 I can remember some of them (40%–80%)					
M7 I can remember most of them (81%–100%)					

FOLLOWING INSTRUCTIONS
When we have to follow the teacher's
instructions

	pupil's opinion	teacher's opinion
M8 I listen and follow		
M9 I do not always follow the instructions		

Experiences of the Mathematics Department

Table 7.4: continued

Name_____

	pupil's opinion	teacher's opinion
PRESENTATION OF WORK		
M10 I find it hard to set out my work in an orderly way		
M11 I present my work in an orderly way if I try		
M12 I organise and present my work in an orderly manner		
USING TIME		
M13 I need a lot of time to do things		
M14 I take a lot of time before settling to work		
M15 I make good use of time in lessons		
M16 I need a lot of time but make good use of it in lessons		
M17 I settle to work quickly, but lose concentration easily		

The pieces of work I did especially well this year were

....

....

Next year I should like to improve...............................

My aural test result was ....%

My examination result was ....% and the examination

average for the year group was ....%.

Signed...

167

Chapter Eight

AN EVALUATION

As the reader has seen, we have taken a whole school approach to profiling which has involved many people - teachers, pupils and their parents - in the process. From the teacher's point of view, there has been much thinking about or rethinking of our educational beliefs, values and attitudes, clarification of what we are hoping to achieve in our lessons, changes in the relationship between the teacher and pupil, and a tentative feeling that we are moving forward. Mingling in with these feelings however, are the doubts which arise from experiencing the problems of implementing such change, and from knowing that for some teachers, this has been a change for which they were philosophically unready, and for which the limited amount of INSET was insufficient. There is also an awareness that, for all of us, a need exists for more training on assessment and particularly on negotiation skills, for more time to think and to talk, and for a release from pressures of all the other initiatives and expectations with which teachers are having to cope at the moment. This latter need is more of an unattainable wish, and is, of course, totally unrealistic as it would be impossible to distance oneself from all the other things - including actually preparing work, teaching and marking it - which are the 'raison d'etre' of schools.

Since so much work has already been done on this project, and bearing in mind the possibility of our future training needs, it is essential that an effective evaluation should take place to inform our thinking and planning. According to Bell (in Bell, Carter and Harris, 1981), evaluation involves the intentional and planned collection of information so that informed judgements can be made about the worth of something. Evaluation based within an institution, may include:

(a) identification of issues of interest and concern
(b) collection of information
(c) sorting, analysing and presenting information
(d) using information to make informed judgements about whether or not the changes are worthwhile.

These aspects of evaluation are not necessarily separate and are often related. Some may be carried out simultaneously.

Evaluating must be regarded as a long-term activity. It is not a process which will normally allow an instant judgment to be made at the end of a brief period of intense work, and some issues may be resolved only after months or even years of careful effort.

I decided to adopt an action research approach to evaluating our project as this would help to formalise the process of studying, analysing, and working out appropriate action designed to improve whatever we found to be the presenting problems. Stenhouse (1975), in discussing educational research, referred to the need of teachers to study their own practice in order to develop a progressive understanding of their work, and Elliott (1981) defined action research as

... the study of a social situation with a view to improving the quality of action within it. The validity of the 'theories' it generates depends not so much on 'scientific' tests of truth, as on their usefulness in helping people to act more intelligently and skilfully ... 'theories' are not validated independently and then applied to practice. They are validated through practice.

It says much for the extended professionalism of our staff (Hoyle, 1972a and 1972c; Stenhouse, op.cit.) that there were plenty of volunteers to take part in the action research project despite the pressures on teachers to complete this term's work and to prepare for the next during the last few weeks of term. We met together and discussed how, within the competing pressures of the rest of our work, we could set about evaluating the profiling which was now nearly complete for the term. We considered the merits of questionnaires, discussion groups, semi-structured interviews, impressionistic prose, and so on, but eventually decided that for the staff we would use a mixture of questionnaire and semi-structured interview, and for the children, discussion groups in lessons. The aim was to take an overview of what had been undertaken, leaving departments to engage in their own more specific evaluation processes.

The staff evaluation was drawn up on the basis of the action research committee discussions, and members of this group each agreed to see two or three other teachers and talk through the informal interviews with them, having asked them to fill in the first part of the document on their own (Table 8.1). While this was going on, a few teachers undertook the evaluation with the pupils through group discussion with individual classes. It had been intended to do this with each of the five First Year classes, but, when it became clear that we had reached saturation where 'no additional data are being found ... (to) develop properties of the category' (Glaser and Strauss, 1967), we decided that the data we had generated was repeating itself to the extent that it was not adding anything more to our observations, but was reinforcing those that had already been made. The mass of data from staff and pupils has yet to be analysed and acted upon following a meeting of the committee, but many departments have already come to a clear understanding of what they would like to change through their own experiences and are putting into practice some of their ideas. An example of this was seen in the mathematics department as described in the last chapter. From a management point of view, it is necessary to have a global view of

(a) what happened
(b) what was liked
(c) what needs to be changed

so that, as R. King has said (in Burgess, 1984), we can seek to 'explain the patterns of social behaviour of real people ... (to be) empirical not speculative, analytical rather than critical, and (to) attempt to avoid value-judgements rather than to make them'.

We collected an impressive amount of data from the pupils, much of which was validated by the fact that it was repeated in each discussion. For the purposes of clarity, I have grouped the comments into those mainly concerned with the teacher, those concerned particularly with the pupil, and those which are essentially about pupil/teacher interaction - although it should be remembered that all the comments arise as a result of the interaction and the relationship between the teacher and pupil. The responses were as follows.

What did you like about the profiling process?

talking with the teachers,

- because you know what is being thought and said about you
- because you find out what they think you have achieved
- because you find out how you've really seemed to them
- on a one to one basis, so that others are not all listening
- as you go along, instead of when it's all over at the end of term
- because it's an opportunity for the teacher to encourage you
- because they can find out what you think
- because it made you feel they cared about you

For yourself

- you can give your opinion - and say what you think
- you can decide for yourself
- you find out what you're good at
- you think about what you might aim for next year
- it helps us to be more realistic
- it's nice to discuss in groups, as friends usually know how you work, and the teacher usually agreed
- it's nice to think it's our own, but would like to write comments on it.

For both pupil and teacher

- you can have out in the open what you both think and feel
- some teachers negotiated with us during the dinner

171

break which made us think they really cared about us and that talking to us was important

From an administrative point of view, I was particularly pleased to be told that the profiles 'were set out neatly and spaced out well' and I felt that what we were doing must really have had an impact if

(a) pupils felt it was all right to comment on the teacher's work, and
(b) that one of the aspects of 'presentation of work' was being applied by pupils outside the confines of profiles about themselves.

The other aspect of the evaluation as far as the children were concerned was their response to the question

What would you change another time?

administrative points

- folders too large to carry around - should be smaller
- folders not strong enough - need hard-backed files
- need ring binders for ease of use
- folders/files could be in House colours to be attractive and encourage sense of belonging to House
- want to keep it looking nice
- needs index and numbered pages
- not given enough time to put profile sheets back in folder, so it all gets out of hand

Changes needed in the process of profiling
Some parts of negotiation were unsatisfactory because

- some teachers - not many - would not listen to/accept our point of view
- some teachers do not know you well enough
- it was too rushed
- some teachers took 'too long' (?) with others in negotiation, so it was boring for the rest
- teachers need to give us examples of evidence
- some teachers are strict and it is hard to say what you think to them
- we didn't have enough courage in saying what we think

- we sometimes weren't able to say what we think firmly and politely
- we agreed too easily if the teacher suggested something different
- we did not feel very pleased if we had to change the level (of skill)
- the teacher's and pupil's point of view should both be recorded if negotiation does not end in agreement

Points other than negotiation

- there was too much profiling all at one time
- some teachers spent too long explaining it
- we should write our own aims, not those the teacher tells you to write.

This mass of data needs to be looked at by the action research committee, so that hypotheses can be advanced. Some of the data is contradictory, in particular that the negotiation was liked by most of the children but, and this was one of the teacher's main problems, the time it took meant that the rest of the class had to get on by themselves, which they were not good at - used to? - doing.

The evaluation does seem to show the following

1. that the children liked the (perceived) change in the teacher/pupil relationship - talking, listening, caring
2. that the pupils liked to know what the teacher (and others) thought about them and valued the insight on themselves
3. that it helped pupils to be more realistic about themselves and to decide on future aims
4. that certain specific administrative matters need attention and could probably be changed without too much difficulty
5. that the process should be spaced out throughout the year
6. that individual teacher/pupil negotiation, whilst welcomed by the individual at the time, seemed to mean boredom for others
7. that teachers must get to know their pupils well if negotiation is to mean anything
8. that negotiation is a skill, and as such would respond to training - both for pupils in their tutorial work programme, and for teachers in specialised INSET.

The evaluation by members of staff corresponded very closely to that of the children, in that they experienced the more personal nature of the relationships, and they felt that the pupils enjoyed talking and finding out about themselves. Spacing the profiling out through the year should be a priority, which had always been intended, but as we had to start somewhere to attain our target of a different report for each first year pupil, it had to be this way for this year. Obviously, as has been discussed before, the integration of profiling to the curriculum is an essential feature of what we hope to achieve, and maybe, through our experiences this year in which we have been less able to cope with such organisation, we will have come to see the absolute necessity for it in the future. The difficulties in negotiation, both in developing the skill involved, and also in the class management during negotiation, were manifest in the many requests for INSET in negotiation skills.

All these points have been touched on in the children's evaluation; the staff also brought into the arena for change the skills to be assessed and the levels of skill achieved. These were largely distinctive departmental problems which were not necessarily shared between all subjects. Some felt that their skills were inappropriate, some that the levels were too high, so that the lowest could not be achieved by the least able, nor the highest by the most able! Some departments needed more categories, some needed them to be more hierarchical, some more discriminatory, some clearer, some differently worded and so on. These will be matters for departments to sort out through discussion amongst themselves, but in order to do so, they will need to look carefully at what they are teaching, what they want to assess, and how and when they want to assess it. Thoughts and ideas generated by other departments will be useful, even if other people cannot actually plan the profile for them. It is here that part of the strength of the working party lies, because although formal discussion can and does trigger thought, the informal discussion and wider staff relationships in the staff room which develop from membership of such a group can prove invaluable.

Other suggestions from staff evaluations were that the profiles should be printed on both sides of the paper, that there was a need to involve the children in understanding the subject skills and the aims of individual lessons, and that one or two other members of staff would have liked to be more involved in the planning of the profiles in the first place. The INSET needs of staff were clearly and loudly identified as learning how to cope with negotiation and in developing negotiation skills.

The evaluation interviews with several members of staff showed how far their thinking had developed during the process of implementing records of achievement. One pointed out that 'it changed my method of teaching so that I was more conscious of making sure the girls understood "the point" of each exercise ... (the work we did) helped the girls to realise that there was not necessarily a right answer in technology and the ideas were shared by the class'. Later, the same member of staff said of her second year syllabus, 'we have changed it with a view to assessment by self-assessment procedures. There will be seven modules which will each have an assessment and an evaluation ... We are in the process of discussing the skills we wish to evaluate, making sure that all of them can be assessed and are reasonably balanced throughout the seven modules.'

Another teacher said that one of the positive things she got out of doing the record of achievement with her classes was that it had focused her thinking on 'what you are teaching and how you teach it. Because of the on-going nature of the project, we can look ahead and plan our curriculum to include a systematic development of our skills over the first three years. We are rethinking our syllabus and will accommodate the profiling principle into our new one.' Yet another member of staff talked of reassessing what she is teaching to move away from a knowledge based pedagogy to 'skills based teaching'.

One further area of evaluation involves the administration of the scheme. There was a great need for time to discuss skills, assessment, criteria, and negotiation, and in the event, there is only so much time in the day which can be used. I am sure that what time was available was used to its potential, but the fact that a limit exists delineated the boundaries of what was possible and the rest had to remain unsaid, or even, unnegotiated. The time expended in the clerical work of producing the profiles, punching holes in them, and collating them was excessive and would need to be radically revised for another year, in which there would be not just one year's profiles but two. There are further problems to be solved regarding inputting to the computer, but compared to the major changes which we have tackled regarding philosophy, pedagogy and educational processes, these could be considered to be relatively minor and purely administrative in nature.

So, where do we go from here?

We need to ensure that the records of achievement working party will continue to meet and discuss issues of importance as they arise, including the report of the action research committee; that feelings and thoughts will continue to be voiced freely; that they will plan and prioritise a course of action informed by our evaluation observations, and that the working party will remain representative of as many subject and personal and social skill areas as seems appropriate. The working party will have to press for the necessary INSET to enable the staff to do the work properly, and there might be benefits to be gained from looking at assessment from a developmental point of view. Novel ideas such as involving children and parents in the planning stages of the profiles could also be discussed, along with the possibility of spreading out throughout the year the production, for each of the different years, of the summative documents which record achievement, thereby distributing the workload more evenly.

It is worth noting the cryptic reminders by P. Easen (1985) of a couple of 'Murphy's Laws', namely, that 'if you try to please everybody, somebody is not going to like it' and 'what ever you want to do, you have to do something else first'. It would seem that these have applied particularly to our experience of profiling, as certainly we have never been able to please everybody, and in not being able to do so, have worried, perhaps unnecessarily, about what we have decided to do. It also seems inevitable that, in order to become more skilled at some of the processes involved, such as assessing and negotiating, we really need good, substantial experience of having done it first!

Nevertheless, the prevailing view amongst heads of department was that they would not wish to effect a moratorium on the work we are doing, and they declared their support for the project to move into a second year. The advent of records of achievement has meant that, in some subject areas, there have been fundamental changes in the delivery of the curriculum or, if teachers have not yet moved that far, many are committed to rethinking and planning for the future to fit in with the philosophy espoused by this innovation. The prospects for the development of the curriculum are indeed exciting, and this, combined with the consequent staff development, will deliver an education which embraces the 'whole person' approach to the development of our children.

Table 8.1: Record of Achievement Evaluation

Name _____ Subject _____

1) How many First Year classes do you teach? 　[   ]
2) How many lessons do you have with each class
per week? 　[   ]
3) How many subject specific skills were on your
list 　[   ]
4) Do you think this is a manageable number for a
First Year RoA? 　[   ]
5) Did you think three levels of skills were usually
appropriate? 　[   ]
6) If no, would you like to comment further?

   ....

   ....

7) How many lessons did you spend, per class, talking
through skills and ticking boxes? 　[   ]
8) How many lessons did you spend on negotiation (per
class)? 　[   ]
9) What did the rest of the class do whilst negotiation
was taking place?

   ....

   ....

10) What three/four things would you change for next
year — please prioritise them

1
2
3
4

11) Do you need — help/advice/opportunity to talk
through — how you could change these? 　[   ]

Table 8.1: continued

Informal Interviews

1) How did you feel about your subject specific skills?

2) What did you feel about the categories/levels of skills?

3) What positive things did you get out of doing this Record of Achievement?

4) What did you think the girls got out of it?

5) Can you suggest departmental ways forward to improve the practice for next year?

6) Can you suggest how you will effect improvements on, for example, your organisation/class management/negotiation strategies/management of time?

7) Can you identify INSET needs to help you for next year? (e.g. negotiation skills; adaptation of curriculum to accommodate spread of achievement etc.)

Thank you for your help in answering these questions.

BIBLIOGRAPHY

Bell, C.D., Carter, J.E.H and Harris, N.D.C. (1981),
   Signposts for Evaluation: a Resource Pack, London,
   Schools Council
Bloom, B.S. (ed) (1956), Taxonomy of Educational
   Objectives, New York, McKay
Bolam, R. (1982), School-Focussed In-Service Training,
   London, Heinemann Educational Books
Brandes, D. and Ginnis, P. (1986) A Guide to Student-
   Centred Learning, Oxford, Blackwell
Bruner, J. (1966), Towards a Theory of Instruction,
   Belknap Press of Harvard University, Mass.
Bullock, A. (1975), Language for Life, London, HMSO
Burgess, R. (ed) (1984), The Research Process in Educational
   Settings, London, Falmer Press
Cockroft, W.H. (1982), Mathematics Counts, London, HMSO
DES (1984), Records of Achievement: A Statement of
   Policy, London, HMSO
Dewey, J. (1916) Democracy and Education
Dewey, J. (1938) Experience and Education
Easen, P. (1985), Making School-Centred INSET Work,
   London, Open University with Croom Helm
Elliott, J. (1981) Action Research: A Framework for Self
   Evaluation in School, Schools Council Programme No. 2
Eraut, M. (1972) In-service Education for Innovation,
   Council for Educational Technology
Glaser, B. and Strauss, A. (1967), The Discovery of Grounded
   Theory, New York, Aldine
Halpin, A.W. (1967), Change and Organisational Climate,
   Journal of Ed. Admin. 5(1), 2-25
Halpin, A.W. (1966), Theory and Research in Administration,

New York, Macmillan

Handy, C. (1976) Understanding Organisations, Harmondsworth, Penguin

Havelock, R. (1973) Planning for Innovation through Dissemination and Utilisation of Knowledge, Michigan, Ann Arbor

HMI (1977), Ten Good Schools, London, HMSO

Holt, J. (1964), How Children Fail, Harmondsworth, Penguin

Hopkins, D. (1985), A Teacher's Guide to Classroom Research, Milton Keynes, Open University Press

Hoy, W.K. and Miskel, C.G. (1978), Educational Administration: Theory, Research & Practice, New York, Random House

Hoyle, E. (1972a) Creativity in the School, OECD Workshop, Estoril, Portugal

Hoyle, E. (1972c) Facing the Difficulties, Bletchley, The Open University

Hoyle, E. (1986) The Politics of School Management, London, Hodder and Stoughton

Hughes, M., Ribbens, P. and Thomas, H. (1985) Managing Education, London, Holt, Rinehart and Winston

Kelly, A.V. (1986), Knowledge and Curriculum Planning, London, Harper & Row

MacDonald, B. in Hamingson, D. (ed) (1973a), Towards Judgment: Humanities Curriculum Project, Norwich, CARN

Mansell, J. in Broadfoot, P. (ed) (1986), Profiles and Records of Achievement, London, Holt, Rinehart and Winston

Maslow, A. (1954), Motivation and Personality, New York, Harper and Row

McGregor, D. (1960), The Human Side of Enterprise, New York, McGraw-Hill Book Co.

McLaughlin, M.W. (1976), Implementation as Mutual Adaptation: Change in Classroom Organisation, Teachers College Record, vol. 77, no. 3, pp.339-51

Nelson-Jones, A. (1983), Practical Counselling Skills, London, Holt, Rinehart and Winston

Peters, R.S. in Archambault, R.D. (1965), Philosophical Analysis and Education, London, Routledge and Kegan Paul

Rogers, C. (1969) Freedom to Learn; a view of what education might become, Merrill, Columbus

Rutter, M., Maughan, B., Mortimore, P. and Ouston, J. (1979), Fifteen Thousand Hours, Shepton Mallet, Open

Books

Schmuck, R. in Bush, T., Glatter, R., Goodey, J. and Riches, C. (1980), Approaches to School Management, London, Harper and Row

Stenhouse, L. (1975), An Introduction to Curriculum Research and Development, London, Heinemann

Taylor, W. in Horton, T. and Raggatt, P. (1982), Challenge and Change in the Curriculum, London, Hodder and Stoughton

Telfer, in Zaltman, Florio and Sikorski (1977), Dynamic Educational Change, Free Press/Macmillan